Salesforce Reporting and Dashboards

Master the art of building successful reports and dashboards with this comprehensive guide

Johan Yu

PUBLISHING

BIRMINGHAM - MUMBAI

Salesforce Reporting and Dashboards

First published: March 2015

Production reference: 1240315

Published by Packt Publishing Ltd.
Livery Place
35 Livery Street
Birmingham B3 2PB, UK.

ISBN 978-1-78439-467-7

www.packtpub.com

Credits

Author
Johan Yu

Reviewers
Chamil Madusanka

Jeff May

Acquisition Editor
Sonali Vernekar

Content Development Editor
Natasha Dsouza

Technical Editor
Sebastian Rodrigues

Copy Editor
Vikrant Phadke

Project Coordinator
Akash Poojary

Proofreaders
Simran Bhogal

Maria Gould

Paul Hindle

Indexer
Rekha Nair

Production Coordinator
Nitesh Thakur

Cover Work
Nitesh Thakur

Foreword

We are in the middle of one of the most exciting times for business and technology, with technological change happening at an unprecedented rate. Everything is getting smarter—cars (self-driving cars), houses (self-regulated houses), hospitals (smart medical devices), shops (1:1 marketing)—and we are moving to "systems of intelligence", but the customer remains at the center. Companies need to be smarter for their customers—connecting the dots and building more intelligence for sales, service, marketing, analytics, communities, apps, and so on. Salesforce's customer success platform will take customers there.

Customers and devices are being connected in a way that was unimaginable a decade ago, and as they do so, a large amount of data is created. Every customer, including you, expects a better service, personalized by knowledge of every interaction with every business or organization. All of these customer connections require a customer-focused technology platform to manage these interactions.

Founded in 1999, Salesforce, the customer success platform and the world's #1 CRM company, empowers companies to connect with their customers in a whole new way. It allows companies to grow sales faster, deliver customer service everywhere, create 1:1 marketing journeys, engage with customers in interactive communities, deliver analytics for every business user, and create custom apps that run on any device. All of these interactions create large volumes of data, which organizations need to be able to view and report on in real time. At its core, Salesforce also has a powerful dashboard and reporting capability, allowing you to view that data in real time.

Johan Yu, Salesforce MVP in Asia, has a deep understanding and knowledge of Salesforce technology and is instrumental in answering questions from many Salesforce customers through Salesforce communities. This book gives every Salesforce user the power to build dashboards and reports quickly and easily on the Salesforce platform. It provides an explanation of the Salesforce data model, how to manage data in Salesforce, how to create reports and dashboards, and how to work with filters, security, and formulas. Finally, Johan explains how to access all of your Salesforce information on a mobile device using the Salesforce1 mobile app.

This book is aimed at Salesforce administrators, business users, and managers who use Salesforce for their daily work. It will provide you with the expertise to unlock all of the data held in Salesforce, thereby increasing the ability to make effective data-driven decisions. As a result, companies become more customer-centric, more efficient, and ultimately, more successful.

Gary Luton
Vice President, Asia - Customers for Life, Salesforce

About the Author

Johan Yu has more than 17 years of experience working in the IT field across MNCs and leading Salesforce.com consulting companies across the Asia-Pacific region.

Johan has worked on Salesforce technology for more than 10 years. He started his career with the Salesforce technology as a developer, team leader, technical manager, and consultant. He now enjoys working as global Salesforce.com system administrator and solution architect in an MNC.

Based in Singapore, Johan holds multiple Salesforce certifications, including Administrator, Advanced Administrator, Sales Cloud Consultant, and Developer. In his spare time, he enjoys writing blogs related to Salesforce technology (`http://simplysfdc.blogspot.com`) and answering questions in the Salesforce success community.

In May 2014, Johan became the first Salesforce MVP from Singapore and also the first in Southeast Asia. He is also a co-leader of the Salesforce Singapore user group and is keen to help members solve issues related to the Salesforce, such as implementation, adoption, and technical issues.

You can connect with him on Twitter at `@simplysfdc`.

Acknowledgments

First of all, I am grateful to the almighty God for enabling me to complete this book. After living and breathing with Salesforce technologies for more than a decade in my career, it's a miracle and my happiest moment to write a book that I am passionate about.

I would like to thank Salesforce for the invention of such a great technology. Thanks to Matt Brown and the entire Salesforce MVP community, where we live as a big family in the Watercooler. I wish to express my sincere gratitude to my MVP fellow Jeff May for completing the review and feedback of this book and Chamil Madusanka for his input.

I also would like to thank the Salesforce Singapore user group leaders for their support: Gary Luton, CK Fong, Kevin Wee, Lena Ser, Paul Rickleton, and Vladimir Vujatovic. Another big thanks to the team from Packt Publishing for their guidance and support that made this book happen.

I also would like to thank my employer, church, family, and friends. Thanks Ps. Jacub Suria, minister of Indonesian Family Church, Singapore, for his down-to-earth kindness and passion in giving all of us sermons and tasty food! Lastly, huge thanks and love to my wife, Novida Lunardi, for being part of my life. Her understanding, continued support, and encouragement helped me get this book completed.

About the Reviewers

Chamil Madusanka is a Salesforce.com-certified Force.com developer. He has been working on Force.com projects since 2011. He has worked as a developer on many custom applications built on Force.com and has also trained end users and new Salesforce developers in his current company, attune Lanka, and former company, Sabre Technologies. He authored *Visualforce Developer's Guide*. His second book was *Learning Force.com Application Development*.

Chamil is an active member of the Force.com community and has contributed to the Force.com community through various channels. He is keen about Force.com and shares his knowledge on Force.com technologies through his blog at http://salesforceworld.blogspot.com/. On the Force.com discussion board, he shares his knowledge and experience on Force.com by providing effective solutions to developer questions. He is the initiator and the organizer of the Sri Lanka Salesforce Platform Developer user group. He organized the first ever Sri Lanka Salesforce Mini Hackathon in 2014. His contribution to the Sri Lankan Salesforce community has led to an increase in Salesforce competency in Sri Lanka.

Chamil completed his BSc in computer science from the University of Colombo, School of Computing, Sri Lanka (UCSC). His areas of interest include cloud computing, semantic web technologies, and ontology-based systems. His other interests include reading technology books and technology blog posts and playing cricket. Chamil can be reached via Twitter (@chamilmadusanka), Skype (chamilmadusanka), and e-mail (chamil.madusanka@gmail.com).

Jeff May is an independent consultant and Salesforce MVP. He specializes in small business deployments and the adoption of Salesforce.com and related business processes. His clients rely on his 25-year-long software engineering and business background to help them clarify their business goals, identify technology needs, and design and deploy effective and scalable Salesforce configurations to support their goals. When he's not working with clients, you can find him on the Salesforce success community, collaborating with other admins and users. You can learn more about Jeff and his business at www.misstheiceberg.com.

www.PacktPub.com

Support files, eBooks, discount offers, and more

For support files and downloads related to your book, please visit www.PacktPub.com.

Did you know that Packt offers eBook versions of every book published, with PDF and ePub files available? You can upgrade to the eBook version at www.PacktPub.com and as a print book customer, you are entitled to a discount on the eBook copy. Get in touch with us at service@packtpub.com for more details.

At www.PacktPub.com, you can also read a collection of free technical articles, sign up for a range of free newsletters and receive exclusive discounts and offers on Packt books and eBooks.

https://www2.packtpub.com/books/subscription/packtlib

Do you need instant solutions to your IT questions? PacktLib is Packt's online digital book library. Here, you can search, access, and read Packt's entire library of books.

Why subscribe?

- Fully searchable across every book published by Packt
- Copy and paste, print, and bookmark content
- On demand and accessible via a web browser

Free access for Packt account holders

If you have an account with Packt at www.PacktPub.com, you can use this to access PacktLib today and view 9 entirely free books. Simply use your login credentials for immediate access.

Instant updates on new Packt books

Get notified! Find out when new books are published by following @PacktEnterprise on Twitter or the *Packt Enterprise* Facebook page.

Table of Contents

Preface

This book is for Salesforce.com administrators, business users, and managers who use Salesforce.com in their daily work or to analyze data. It covers all items related to reporting and dashboards in Salesforce. This book will benefit business users, who will gain knowledge ranging from creating basic reports in Salesforce to advanced report and dashboard configuration. Administrators will learn the entire concept of reporting and dashboards, object models, permissions related to reports and dashboards, report storage, and enabling historical data setup.

Reports and dashboards are among the most powerful and easiest-to-use features in the Salesforce platform, including Sales Cloud, Service Cloud, and Force.com, where business users are able to create and customize reports and dashboards as needed in minutes.

Business users should have basic knowledge (or should be using Salesforce.com in their daily work), such as logging in to the system, navigation through Salesforce, creating and editing data, and running reports in Salesforce. Admin users should have basic knowledge in customizing Salesforce, such as the setup menu, tabs, user profiles, permission sets, and standard and custom objects.

What this book covers

Chapter 1, *Introducing Salesforce.com*, provides a basic overview of the Salesforce object model, setup menu navigation, and using Schema Builder to understand objects and fields.

Chapter 2, *Managing Data in Salesforce.com*, starts with multiple ways of backing up Salesforce data, Sandbox, and data import. This chapter ends by covering data visibility and accessibility.

Chapter 3, *Creating Your First Report*, discusses report folders, permissions, report types, and report creation from scratch.

Chapter 4, *Working with Reports*, covers multiple types of report formats, adding charts to reports, report filters, advanced report types, and subscribing to a report.

Chapter 5, *Learning Advanced Report Configuration*, discusses categorizing data in reporting, custom summary formulas, scheduling reports, and adding embedded report charts.

Chapter 6, *Creating Your First Dashboard*, covers dashboard permissions, dashboard folders, dashboard components, integrating dashboards with Chatter, and the creation of a dashboard from scratch.

Chapter 7, *Learning Advanced Dashboard Configuration*, explains the advanced functionalities in dashboards, including dashboard filters, dynamic dashboards, drill-down, and additional dashboards from AppExchange.

Chapter 8, *Accessing Historical Data*, covers multiple options used to enable and access historical data in Salesforce without additional third-party applications.

Chapter 9, *Dashboards and Reports in Salesforce1*, shows you how to access reports and dashboards on the go using the Salesforce1 mobile app.

What you need for this book

The best approach to get the most of this book is to get hands-on experience of all the exercises. You will need the following:

- A Salesforce account. You are advised to use the Enterprise edition and above. But for the purpose of testing, the Sandbox instance and Developer edition are good enough.
- A web browser.
- An Internet connection.
- A computer.
- A mobile phone, iOS, or Android smartphone.

Who this book is for

This book is written for business analysts, reporting analysts, sales representatives, sales operations, and Salesforce administrators. This book is also for users who want to learn about Salesforce reporting and dashboards in depth. You will gain knowledge of items related to reports and dashboards in Salesforce, starting from creating basic reports and customizing them to the most advanced reports using Salesforce.

Conventions

In this book, you will find a number of styles of text that distinguish between different kinds of information. Here are some examples of these styles, and an explanation of their meaning.

Code words in text, database table names, folder names, filenames, file extensions, pathnames, dummy URLs, user input, and Twitter handles are shown as follows: "You can relate an object to other objects in Salesforce.com, for example, relating the Expense custom object to the Project custom object."

New terms and **important words** are shown in bold. Words that you see on the screen, in menus or dialog boxes for example, appear in the text like this: "You can sign up and get the Developer edition for free by clicking on **Sign Up** at https://developer.salesforce.com/page/Developer_Edition."

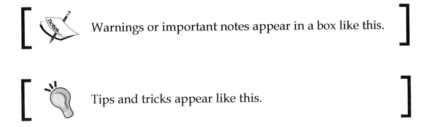

Warnings or important notes appear in a box like this.

Tips and tricks appear like this.

Reader feedback

Feedback from our readers is always welcome. Let us know what you think about this book—what you liked or may have disliked. Reader feedback is important for us to develop titles that you really get the most out of.

To send us general feedback, simply send an e-mail to `feedback@packtpub.com`, and mention the book title via the subject of your message.

If there is a topic that you have expertise in and you are interested in either writing or contributing to a book, see our author guide on `www.packtpub.com/authors`.

Customer support

Now that you are the proud owner of a Packt book, we have a number of things to help you to get the most from your purchase.

Errata

Although we have taken every care to ensure the accuracy of our content, mistakes do happen. If you find a mistake in one of our books—maybe a mistake in the text or the code—we would be grateful if you would report this to us. By doing so, you can save other readers from frustration and help us improve subsequent versions of this book. If you find any errata, please report them by visiting `http://www.packtpub.com/submit-errata`, selecting your book, clicking on the **erratasubmissionform** link, and entering the details of your errata. Once your errata are verified, your submission will be accepted and the errata will be uploaded on our website, or added to any list of existing errata, under the Errata section of that title. Any existing errata can be viewed by selecting your title from `http://www.packtpub.com/support`.

Piracy

Piracy of copyright material on the Internet is an ongoing problem across all media. At Packt, we take the protection of our copyright and licenses very seriously. If you come across any illegal copies of our works, in any form, on the Internet, please provide us with the location address or website name immediately so that we can pursue a remedy.

Please contact us at copyright@packtpub.com with a link to the suspected pirated material.

We appreciate your help in protecting our authors, and our ability to bring you valuable content.

Questions

You can contact us at questions@packtpub.com if you are having a problem with any aspect of the book, and we will do our best to address it.

1
Introducing Salesforce.com

This chapter will give you a general introduction to **Salesforce.com**. You will learn the benefits of cloud computing technology and how to extend beyond the Salesforce CRM application using custom objects. There is also an introduction to Schema Builder. Then we will be covering the Salesforce.com architecture, setup menu, and testing environment. This guide will involve some hands-on activities for mastering reports and dashboard creation from *Chapter 3*, *Creating Your First Report*, and onwards.

This chapter contains information about reporting and dashboards that applies to both business users and system administrators. Some topics in this chapter discuss features specific for system administrators, but business users will also find it interesting to understand the Salesforce.com architecture better.

Throughout this chapter, we will provide notes and tips for you to understand the Salesforce.com technology. The following topics will be covered in this chapter:

- Overview and benefits of Salesforce.com
- The Salesforce object model
- Navigating the setup menu
- Schema Builder

Overview and benefits of Salesforce.com

Salesforce.com is a web-based enterprise platform that you can access from anywhere, anytime, and on any device as long as you are connected to the Internet. It is a cloud application, so you do not need to purchase any server/hardware, operating system, or database to use it. If you haven't used Salesforce.com before, then let me tell you that it is a web-based application like Gmail or Yahoo e-mail, but it takes this a step further because it allows you to configure and customize it to suit your business needs.

When you sign up for Salesforce, you will be provided with an "organization," which is basically a software environment. Hardware, the operating system, and the database are shared among Salesforce customers within the same "instance". Salesforce customers within the same instance run the same version of platform.

You can illustrate the Salesforce platform as an apartment building, shared by many residences. In this multitenant environment, each organization's data, configuration, and users are completely isolated and are not accessible to any other organization. So, when you configure your Salesforce organization, the metadata changes are only for your organization. A similar rule applies to your database; access to it is only for your registered users.

If you have heard about cloud computing, you will easily understand that since Salesforce.com is a **Software as a Service (SaaS)** model, you will only need to configure Salesforce.com to start using it. Everything from object model and business logic to page layouts, reports, and dashboards is provided by the Salesforce platform. It also has its own Java-like programming language called Apex, and an HTML-like visual markup language called Visualforce page for custom user interface design.

Since the Salesforce team takes care of the infrastructure, maintenance, software upgrades, backup, and performance, it benefits companies by lowering the IT cost and the cost of resources. As a Salesforce subscriber, you just need to maintain your users and implement the business processes you need.

When Mark Benioff started Salesforce.com from his apartment in San Francisco back in 1997, Salesforce.com was intended to act as a CRM application only. However, as the platform grew and became more robust, Salesforce opened up its platform to more customization, where you could build any kind of applications beyond CRM.

The following products are available in this platform at the time of writing this book:

- **Sales Cloud**: This is used to automate your sales process
- **Service Cloud**: This is used to deliver revolutionary customer service process
- **Marketing Cloud**: This is used to provide digital marketing automation
- **Analytics Cloud**: This is used to deliver analytics for business users and analysts
- **Force.com platform**: This allows you to build your own Enterprise custom apps that connect with customers, employees, and partners

In summary, the advantages of using Salesforce.com compared to other on-premise applications are as follows:

- Faster implementation schedule
- Lower maintenance cost, since you don't have to buy or support in-house servers, data centers, and high-speed internet connections, or hire any IT staff for this work
- It is scalable and robust
- Security and high performance
- Easily expandable functionality using prebuilt solutions from the AppExchange
- Access from desktops, laptops, and mobile devices with Internet connectivity
- Enjoy enterprise grade level application for small and medium businesses

Salesforce Object Model

Objects are key components in Salesforce.com. They allow you to store your data. Similar to a table in a database, an object consists of several fields to store data. You can set some fields as mandatory, while some other fields such as ID, Created Date, Created By, Last Modified Date, and Last Modified By will be automatically populated by the system.

You can illustrate an object as a table, a field as a column in the table, and a record as a row in the table. In the following table, **field 1** will store the values for all first names, **field 2** will store the values for all birth dates, and so on:

	field 1	**field 2**	**field 3**
record 1	John	29 Jun	...
record 2	May	10 Dec	...
record 3	Steve	24 Feb	...

There are two type of objects in Salesforce:

- Standard object
- Custom object

Standard objects

Standard objects are provided by Salesforce.com by default. Each standard object has its own uniqueness, and the objects are named by their common uses. Some of the main Salesforce.com objects when you subscribe for Sales or Service Cloud are as follows:

- **Account**: This is used to store information about the businesses and organizations your company interacts with.

- **Contact**: This is used to store information about the people associated with your customers.

- **Opportunity**: This is used to store information about sales interactions with your customers. It is often known as the sales cycle.

- **Lead**: This is used to store information about people who may become customers or partners of your company.

- **Case**: This is used to store information about interactions with your customers related to the products or services you provide.

- **Campaign**: This is used to store information about your company's marketing activities and responses.

Some other standard objects are **Activity, Asset, Contract, Quote, Order, Products,** and **Price Book**.

Each standard object comes with default fields based on the purpose of the object, for example, Stage in Opportunity and Mobile Phone in Contact. You can create your own fields in a standard object called custom field. The maximum number of fields you can create depends on the Salesforce edition purchased.

> You can upgrade Salesforce.com to a higher edition simply by paying the increased subscription fee, and continue using the same organization with the existing database and customization. But if you plan to "downgrade" to a lower edition (it is actually not possible to downgrade), Salesforce.com will give you a brand new organization where you will need to reconfigure and transfer all your data.

Custom objects

Custom objects are specific objects created in your organization to store data for your business that does not fit into standard objects. Only a user with admin access is allowed to create custom objects. Most AppExchange packages create and use custom objects, since they provide specific business processes.

The maximum number of custom objects that can be created depends on the Salesforce edition. If you have admin permission, you can create objects and fields in Salesforce with just point-and-click rather than using complex SQL scripts as in traditional databases.

For a standard object, the number of standard fields depends on the object itself, but a custom object comes with a few standard fields that are the same for all custom objects:

- `Id`
- `Name`
- `Created By` and `Created Date`
- `Last Modified By` and `Last Modified Date`
- `Owner` (if the object is not a child of another object in a master-detail relationship)

Just as with a standard object, you can create custom fields in a custom object.

Object relationships

You can relate an object to other objects in Salesforce.com, for example, relating the `Expense` custom object to the `Project` custom object. With this relation, you can know for which project the specific expense is used. In this example, `Project` will be considered as the parent and `Expense` as the child object. Remember that one parent can have many children, while the child can have only one parent. To build this relationship from the child object, create a lookup or master-detail relationship field for the parent object.

There are two types of object relationships in Salesforce.com:

- Master-detail relationship
- Lookup relationship

Here is the comparison between master-detail relationships and lookup relationships:

Master-detail relationship	Lookup relationship
You can define master-detail relationships between custom objects or between a custom object and a standard object (standard object must be the parent).	You can define a relationship between any two objects, standard or custom.
When a record in a master object (parent) is deleted, all the records in the detail object (child) that are related to that master record will be deleted.	When a parent object is being deleted, you can configure a child object to either clear the parent record value in the child record or prevent deletion of the parent record.
All child records must have a related parent record.	The parent record may not require a related parent record.
The ownership of the child record is determined by the related parent record. Child records do not have an owner.	Each child record has an owner and is not related to the parent record.
The detail record inherits sharing and security from the master record.	There is no security or inheritance between related parent and child records.
To relate an object to another object, no records should exist in the child object.	To relate an object to other objects, there is no condition on the number of records.
If you have the Roll-Up Summary field in the parent object, any create, edit, or delete action in the child record will trigger an edit action in the parent object. If you have a validation rule and other rules in parent object, the validation rules will trigger for the parent object.	You cannot create the Roll-Up Summary field in the lookup relationship using out-of-the-box Salesforce functionality.
Supports cross-object workflow. You can configure a field update action to update a field in the parent record using a value from the child record.	Does not support cross-object workflow.

To create a master-detail relationship for an existing object with records as the child object, you can initially define it as a lookup relationship, populate all parent fields for all records, and then change the relationship to a master-detail relationship.

You can build a many-to-many object relationship using two master-detail relationships in a single custom object, which is known as a **junction object** in that case.

Field types

Salesforce.com comes with field data types that fit your business model. Some of them are built with business logic, such as e-mails and URLs, these need to follow valid e-mail and URL formats respectively. Invalid values will be automatically rejected by the system. When you define custom fields, the data type you select determines which additional options you can specify **Required**, **Unique**, **Case sensitive**, **External ID**, and **Default Value**.

Here is the list of Salesforce's data types:

- Auto Number
- Formula
- Roll-Up Summary, if the object is a parent in a master-detail relationship
- Hierarchical Relationship (only for the User object)
- Lookup relationship
- Master-detail relationship
- Checkbox
- Currency
- Date
- Date/Time
- E-mail
- Geolocation
- Number
- Percent
- Picklist
- Picklist (multi-select)
- Text
- Text Area
- Text Area (long)

- Text Area (rich)
- Text (encrypted)
- URL

Sandbox or Developer Edition?

It is advised that you get your hands on all exercises in this book in a Sandbox org or Developer Edition, not in the production environment, as you might change something without knowing.

If you do not have Sandbox org for testing, you can sign up and get Developer Edition for free by clicking on **Sign Up** at `https://developer.salesforce.com/page/Developer_Edition`.

Sandbox has an exact copy of your production configuration on the date of Sandbox creation or Sandbox refreshes. Depending on the Sandbox type, you can have a complete copy of production data, partial data, or no data in a Sandbox, but all of them will have a configuration copy from the production environment. We will discuss more on Sandbox in *Chapter 2, Managing Data in Salesforce.com*.

While Developer Edition is an environment without any relation to your production environment, it is good enough for you to try anything explained in this book.

Navigating the Setup menu

Depending on your user details and by navigating to **Setup | User Interface**, here are a few ways to find the **Setup** menu:

- If the Salesforce instance organization has **Enable Improved Setup User Interface** enabled, the **Setup** link will be visible next to **Help**, as shown in this screenshot:

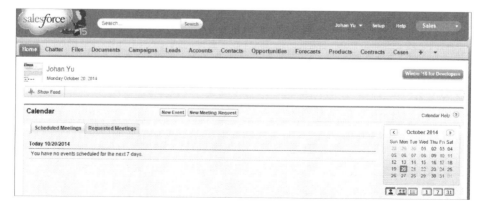

- For a Salesforce instance without **Enable Improved Setup User Interface** enabled, click on your name, and the **Setup** link will appear in the drop-down window shown in the following screenshot:

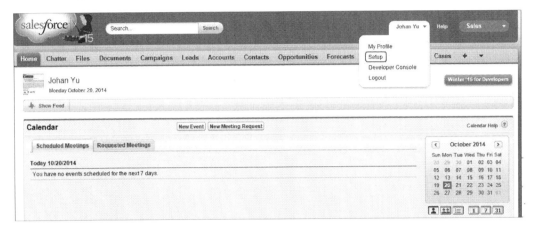

- A Salesforce instance with **Enable Improved Setup User Interface** and **Accessibility Mode** enabled in your user details will look like the following screenshot:

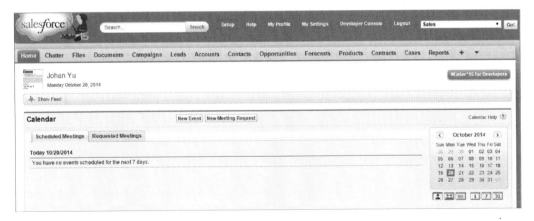

- A Salesforce instance with **Enable Improved Setup User Interface** disabled and **Accessibility Mode** enabled in your user details will look like the following screenshot:

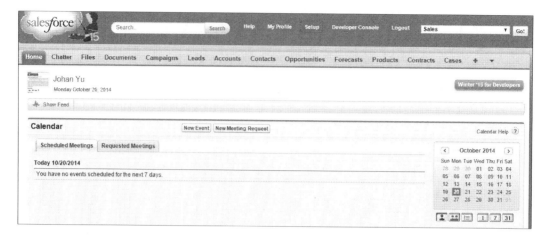

 To find the **Enable Improved Setup User Interface** option, navigate to **Setup** | **Customize** | **User Interface**.

Schema Builder

Schema Builder is a tool within Salesforce.com that is used to view and manage objects, fields, and relations between objects in a graphical interface. It is available in all Salesforce.com editions. Schema Builder is not the only option to view and manage objects, fields, and relations between objects.

The following screenshot shows four custom objects that have been created: **Object1**, **Object2**, **Object3**, and **Object4**. **Object2** and **Object3** have a master-detail relationship with **Object1**, while **Object4** has a lookup relationship with **Object1**.

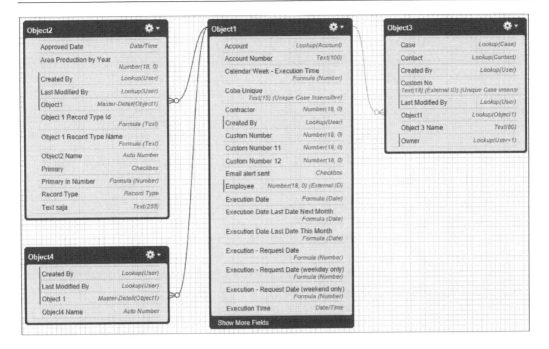

Some users prefer to create the field manually rather than use Schema Builder. Manual field creation offers more options such as field-level security and adding fields to the page layout. To create or access a field, navigate to **Setup | Customize** for standard objects or **Setup | Create | Objects** for custom objects, and then you can configure the object and the field.

Schema Builder in action

Schema Builder will be available only if you have the **Customize Application** permission. Here are a few actions you can perform with Schema Builder:

- Create and delete custom objects
- Edit custom object properties
- Create and delete custom fields

- Edit custom field properties
- Manage custom field permissions

In addition to the preceding actions, with Schema Builder, you can easily:

- Understand fields in an object:
    ◦ Required field and auto-populate field by system mark with red bar before field name
    ◦ Field type, field length, external ID, and unique fields displayed in the right column

- Understand relationships between objects:
    ◦ The one end with circle and arrow is the child object. Remember that one parent can have multiple children.
    ◦ The master-detail relationship is displayed by a red line, while the lookup relationship is displayed by a blue line.

Hands-on – navigating Schema Builder

Once you log in to Salesforce.com, there are three options you can use to open Schema Builder:

1. Navigate to **Setup | Schema Builder**.
2. Go to **Setup | Create | Objects** and click on **Schema Builder** in the panel to the right.
3. Go to **Setup | Home**, and in the **Quick Links** box, click on the **Schema Builder** link.

If you don't see the **Schema Builder** link, it means that your user does not have the permission to customize the application.

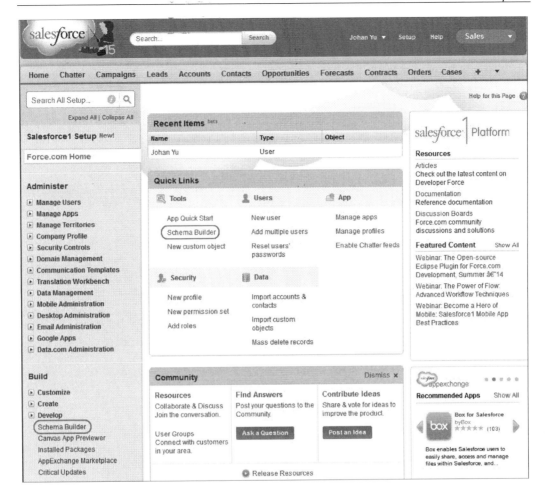

 When you are in the **Setup** page, you can type in the **Search All Setup...** textbox to search for a menu. The system will automatically filter the menu as you type.

Once you are in Schema Builder, you will see the following main tabs in the left menu:

- **Elements**
- **Objects**

Elements will show all field types (except **Geolocation**). You can drag and drop a field onto an object to add new custom fields for that object.

Objects will have an option to show all objects, standard objects, custom objects, system objects, and selected objects.

Hands-on – working in Schema Builder

Select objects that you would like to analyze or work on in the left panel. Selected objects will show up in the main canvas area. Here are a few actions you can perform with Schema Builder:

- To create a new custom object, drag the **Object** icon from the **Elements** tab onto the canvas area. It will prompt you to enter an object label and other required information.

- To create a new custom field, drag a field-type icon from the **Elements** tab onto an object selected in the canvas area. It will prompt you to enter a field label and other required information.

- To move the object in the canvas, click on the object name and drag it.

- Click on the gear icon at the top-right corner of the object. For standard objects, you can:
  - Hide the object.
  - View the object and page layout. It will open the details in a new window.

  For custom objects, click on the icon to:
  - Hide the object.
  - View the object and page layout. It will open the details in a new window.
  - Edit the object properties.
  - Delete the object.

- In the case of standard fields, you can right-click on the field to view it in a new window. For custom fields, you can right-click on the field to:
  - View the field in a new window
  - Edit the field properties
  - Manage field permissions
  - Delete the field

Summary

In this chapter, we started with a discussion on Salesforce.com's architecture, the benefits of using the Salesforce.com technology, and multiple products from Salesforce.com.

We continued to discuss the Salesforce object model, how data is stored, types of objects, and the difference between standard and custom objects. You understood how to relate objects, relationships between objects (master-detail relationships and lookup relationships), and a comparison of both the relationship models. You also learned about multiple field types for objects.

Next, you learned how to find the **Setup** menu, and we covered the testing environment with the Sandbox or Developer Edition to get a hands-on of this book's activities. At the end of this chapter, we went into a little depth about getting a hands-on of Schema Builder. Then you learned how to navigate it to analyze and configure object models.

In the next chapter, we will go through various data management activities including data backup, data import, the Sandbox environment, and data accessibility. This chapter is intended more for system administrators, but business users will nevertheless get more knowledge on how to manage data in Salesforce.

2
Managing Data in Salesforce.com

Data management plays an important role in implementing and maintaining a successful adoption of Salesforce.com in an organization. Using Salesforce reporting and dashboards, you can easily analyze the data stored in most objects. Therefore, bad data will produce a bad result, and the report generated will not be of any use. For this reason, it is very important for you to keep your data clean, complete, and reliable.

In this chapter we will be covering data management in Salesforce, starting with a brief introduction to data backup in Salesforce, how to back up, and why backup is needed. Then we will continue with Sandbox, the types of Sandboxes, and Sandbox refreshing.

Data import is another interesting topic in Salesforce. It shows how we can bring external data into Salesforce regularly or on demand. We will end this chapter with data visibility and accessibility in Salesforce.

Throughout this chapter, we will provide notes and tips to help you understand important items. The topics covered here are:

- Data backup
- Sandbox
- Data import
- Data visibility and accessibility

Much of this chapter is intended for system administrators who need to maintain data in Salesforce. Business users will definitely benefit from understanding how to manage data, the Sandbox environment, and the concepts of data visibility and accessibility in Salesforce.

Back up your data

In general, data backup is an activity of copying data and files from a source to media or devices. When you perform data backup properly, you should be able to restore data from the backup media in the event of data loss, such as device failure. Another purpose of data backup is to recover data from an earlier time because of invalid, deleted data or for audit purposes.

Data loss may cause critical issues and even financial losses for the company. Corporates should have their data backup and restoration planned as per their business needs, and should store the backup in a safe place.

Back up Salesforce data

How about a backup of Salesforce data? Are you able to back it up? Yes, you can back up Salesforce data. Although Salesforce is a cloud application, it does not mean you cannot back up your data and the configuration (metadata) in your local computer or server.

What is the need to back up our Salesforce data? Salesforce handles backup activity and disaster recovery, and as a user we do not need to worry about it when something goes wrong. However, if you do not back up your data, manually or on schedule, you will not have access to historical data. Salesforce always shows the latest data, for example, when your user complains that data is missing, or when your user would like to know an older value from a record but the field is not tracked.

When you back up your data in another location, you can access it offline or from a database.

 You can request Salesforce to provide data on a certain date, but there is a cost for this type of request.

Performing data backup in Salesforce

Salesforce provides a tool for system admin to back up Salesforce data using **Data Export**. **Data Export** lets you prepare a copy of your selected data in Salesforce for you to download. You can use this tool when needed or schedule it.

After going to **Setup | Data Management | Data Export**, you can export data or schedule for weekly or monthly exporting. Once you've clicked on **Export Now** or **Schedule Export**, it will open a new window with the following options:

- **Export File Encoding**
- **Include images, documents, and attachments**
- **Include Chatter files and Salesforce CRM Content document versions**
- **Replace carriage returns with spaces**
- **Schedule Data Export** (if you select **Schedule Export**)
- Include all data or some objects (we have discussed data object in *Chapter 1, Introducing Salesforce.com*)

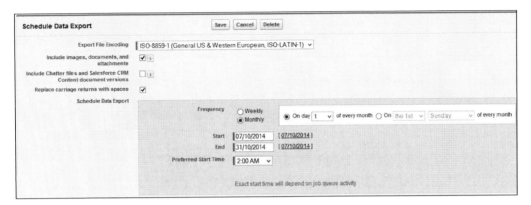

Once the backup data is ready, you will receive an e-mail containing a URL for you to download. It will be in a ZIP file (or files) containing objects selected to back up. The backup files will be available for 48 hours after creation and will be auto-deleted after that. You need to click on the link of the file (or files) to download it to your local computer.

The size of a ZIP file is up to 512 MB. If your data is bigger than 512 MB, in the compress ZIP mode, it will split into many ZIP files, and you need to download them manually. When the file is large, the downloading process may be disrupted and you will need to redownload it again if it fails. It is good practice to extract the files after all files have been downloaded to make sure you can restore them when needed.

Data Export involves manual user activity by clicking to download data every week or month, depending on the frequency scheduled. There are a few other options to back up or synchronize Salesforce data with your backend database:

- AppExchange product; navigate to `https://appexchange.salesforce.com`, search for `backup`, and you will find a few applications such as **Backupify**, **Spanning Backup**, **OwnBackup**, **CloudAlly**, and so on. However, these are not Salesforce products and they are not free.

- Custom data integration with:

  ○ ETL tools, such as Informatica or Informatica Cloud, Jitterbit, Apatar, and so on

  ○ Custom applications using the Force.com API

Playing with Sandbox

A Sandbox in Salesforce is a snapshot of your production environment on the date you create or refresh it. A Sandbox instance is created in a separate environment for a variety of purposes such as development, testing, and training, without affecting the data and configurations in your Salesforce production instance.

Some people may consider Sandbox as a backup of production data and configuration at a point of time, but this is wrong because you usually will use Sandbox for other purposes such as coding, testing, quality assurance, and staging. Sandboxes should not be considered as data backups for the following reasons:

- Full Sandbox refresh is limited to once every 29 days.
- The full Sandbox is only included in the Unlimited and Performance editions. For all others, it has to be purchased as an add-on to your subscription.

The Sandbox should be nearly identical to your production data and configuration. You need to refresh the Sandbox to apply the latest production configuration, data changes, and all existing configurations. Data in the Sandbox that hasn't been deployed in the production environment will be overwritten.

 It is good practice to schedule a Sandbox refresh every month or quarter, depending on your organization's needs. When you have a big deployment, make sure you refresh the Sandbox to get the latest snapshot for support and for troubleshooting if any issues arise.

You may have multiple Sandboxes depending on your licenses or additional Sandbox purchases. Each Sandbox instance is isolated from other instances, so operations performed in one Sandbox will not affect other Sandboxes or your production environment. You can deploy Change Sets from one Sandbox to another Sandbox within the same Production org, also Change Sets are deployed from and to Production with the Sandbox.

Sandbox is only available for Enterprise Edition and above, but you can purchase Sandbox if you are using Professional Edition.

Types of Sandboxes

The different types of Sandboxes are:

- **Developer Sandbox**: This is designed for coding and testing. It only contains the configuration (metadata) of your production environment.

- **Developer Pro Sandbox**: This is similar to Developer Sandbox (designed for coding and testing), but it has a larger storage limit compared to Developer Sandbox. This allows more robust test datasets, allowing the environment to handle more development and quality assurance tasks.

- **Partial Copy Sandbox**: This is designed for testing environments. It can also be used for quality assurance tasks such as user acceptance testing, integration testing, and training. It includes a copy of your production environment configuration and a subset of your production data as defined by the Sandbox template.

- **Full Sandbox**: This supports full performance testing, load testing, and staging in addition to the tasks that you use other Sandboxes for. This Sandbox will have an exact copy of your production environment, including all the data and configurations at the time it was created or refreshed.

Configuring Sandbox

The option to configure Sandbox is only available for a production instance, not a Sandbox instance. Navigate to **Setup | Sandboxes**. You will see list of existing Sandboxes: **Available Sandbox Licenses**, **Sandbox Template**, and **Sandbox History**, as shown in the following screenshot:

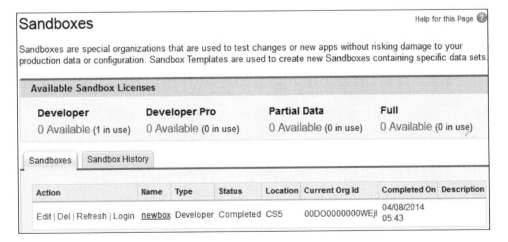

In the screen that you see now, if you still have Sandbox licenses available, you will see the **New Sandbox** button. Then click on **Create** for the Sandbox type you would like to use. Otherwise, you can edit, delete, refresh, or log in to the Sandbox.

Developer and Developer Pro Sandboxes can be refreshed every day, while Partial Data can be refreshed once in 5 days, and Full Sandbox can be refreshed once in 29 days.

Importing data to Salesforce

The ability to import data to Salesforce is important and it may be required quite often, depending on your business. We can split the data import process into manual and automatic. There are a few options to import data into Salesforce. Let's start with the most basic option.

Data Import Wizard

Data Import Wizard is an out-of-the-box tool provided by Salesforce to import accounts/contacts, leads, solutions, and custom objects data to Salesforce. This tool can process up to 50,000 records at a time. If you have a larger volume of data, you can split it into many files, or you can use other tools, which we will be discussing after this topic.

Before launching the wizard, you will need to prepare your data and save it in CSV (comma-separated values) file format. To use this tool, navigate to **Setup | Data Management | Data Import Wizard**:

1. Choose data to import and select the object with any of these actions:
   - **Add new records**
   - **Update existing records**
   - **Add new and update existing records**

   You will have an option to match data with existing data and enable workflow rules.

2. Drag the CSV file onto the wizard screen. You will have an option to select **Character Code**.

3. Next, you need to map the Salesforce object with the CSV file header. Salesforce will perform auto-matching if the column header of the CSV file matches exactly with the object file's label name. The following screenshot shows the page where the mapping is done:

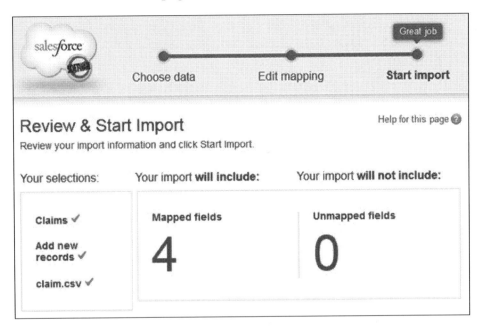

4. Start the import.

5. Follow the preceding steps and click on **Start import**. You can monitor the job status by going to **Setup | Jobs | Bulk Data Load Jobs**. Once importing has been completed, you will get an e-mail notification, with information on the list of successful records created, records updated, and failed records. The e-mail will also contain a URL that will allow you to view the details of the data load job.

Using Data Loader

Data Loader is a desktop application running on the Windows operating system. This tool is built and supported by Salesforce. You can use Data Loader for bulk import, update, and export of data in Salesforce. The available actions in Data Loader include **Insert**, **Update**, **Upsert**, **Delete**, **Export**, and **Export All** from Salesforce.

Export All includes deleted data that is still in **Recycle Bin**, while **Export** does not include deleted data.

You can use Data Loader to move data in and out for most objects in Salesforce, including standard and custom objects. The data format needs to be CSV, and the same format is required when you're exporting data; the output is in the form of CSV files as well.

You need to have API permission in your user details to use Data Loader. Before any action starts, you need to log in to Data Loader. If your profile is not in the login IP range, you will need to add a security token after your password; for example, if your password is `hello123` and the token is `xyx`, you need to enter `hello123xyz` in the password field.

Navigate to **Setup | Data Management | Data Loader** to download the installer. Then click on **Download the Data Loader**. Depending on your web browser, it will download the `ApexDataLoader.exe` installer into your computer, you need to run this file to get it installed on your computer. If you are not an admin user for the computer you log in to, you need to have admin privileges to install this application. The following screenshot shows the Data Loader interface:

You can run Data Loader manually or schedule it to automatically load or extract data to and from Salesforce (respectively). Data Loader is only available for a Windows machine. If you are running Mac OS, search for **LexiLoader** to download and install it. The user interface of LexiLoader is similar to Data Loader.

Partner tools

Additionally, there are a few other tools offered by the Salesforce partner. You can get them for free. They support data import and integration with Salesforce. Since these tools are not built and supported by Salesforce (evaluate thoroughly before using them for your production organization), it is always advised to try them out in the Developer edition or in a Sandbox environment. Navigate to **Setup | Develop | Tools** to get them:

- **Dataloader.io**: This tool is available on the cloud, so nothing needs to be downloaded and installed on your computer. It offers additional features different from the standard Data Loader tool provided by Salesforce.com, such as means to update data in Salesforce with lookup (where you do not need to provide the record ID). The free version does not come with e-mail support and has some limitations compared to the paid version. This tool is good for simple and quick one-off data loads.

- **Informatica Cloud Data Loader**: This is a cloud application as well, but you need to download and install a secure agent on a computer to act as a connection to databases. It supports integration of Salesforce with other cloud applications, on-premise databases, and local files. Informatica Cloud Data Loader also provides a mobile app for iOS and Android devices to monitor the historical activities and usage if you need to perform simple troubleshooting on the go.

- **Jitterbit Data Loader**: To use Jitterbit Data Loader, you need to download and install the application on Windows or Mac OS computers. All tasks need to be configured in the Jitterbit application. Feature-wise, it is almost similar to Informatica Cloud Data Loader. It lets administrators automate import and export of data between flat files, databases, and Salesforce.com. Since this application allows you to configure complex mapping between source and target databases, it is good for scheduling data operations or light integration.

Configure data visibility and accessibility

Salesforce comes with complete functionalities for administrators to configure data secured as per your organization's needs. The way Salesforce works is by setting the object level with less access to all users. If the data needs to be accessible by groups of users, the administrator can configure rules to auto-share it. The other way round is not possible—you cannot give more access to everyone and then create rules to block the access.

There are two fundamental settings that determine user ability to access a record:

- The **Organization-Wide Defaults** (OWD) sharing setting
- User permission

The **Organization-Wide Defaults** (OWD) sharing setting is a fundamental setting for each object in Salesforce that is used to determine object visibility and accessibility. There are a few standard accessibilities that can be configured for each object, although some objects may have special settings. But in general, the default access option is available.

This configuration determines a user's ability to view data in the object, including getting the data into the report. Based on the sharing setting, permission set for the user, user profile permission, and role hierarchy, reports run by a sales manager and a sales representative may have different results. For example, in a private sharing setting for opportunity, a sales manager is able to access all pipelines owned by his subordinates, while a sales representative can only sees their pipeline or pipeline shared with them.

To configure OWD sharing setting for all objects, navigate to **Setup | Security Controls | Sharing Settings**. This will bring up the following screenshot:

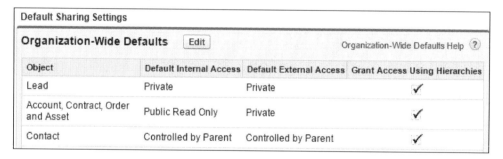

Default Sharing Settings

Object	Default Internal Access	Default External Access	Grant Access Using Hierarchies
Lead	Private	Private	✓
Account, Contract, Order and Asset	Public Read Only	Private	✓
Contact	Controlled by Parent	Controlled by Parent	✓

Permission is a setting related to a user or a group of users. It determines what actions a user can perform, including the ability to access data in objects. The permission is specified in the **Profiles** page and extra permissions can be defined in **Permission Set**.

There are two levels of permission in Salesforce:

- **System Permission**: This permission is related to all objects in your Salesforce environment:
  - **View All Data**: A user with this permission is able to view all of the data regardless of whether the object sharing setting and object permission are enabled or not

- ○ **Modify All Data**: Just like the **View All Data** permission, this user is able to edit all data

- **Object Permission**: This permission is related to the Salesforce object level, not the whole environment:

  - ○ **View All**: A user with this permission is able to view all of the data for that object
  - ○ **Modify All**: This is the same as **View All**, but with the ability to edit data

The following screenshot shows how the object permission setup in the **Profile** page looks if you have not enabled **Enhanced Profile User Interface**:

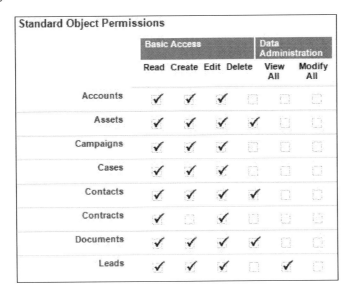

Even the object OWD setting is **Private**, but if the user permission for the object is **View All**, the user will be able to see all the records for that object. For example:

- Lead object sharing setting in **Organization-Wide Defaults** (OWD) is **Private**
- Users have the **View All** permission for the lead object
- The result is that the user is able to see all lead records in the entire organization because of the **View All** permission, although it is **Private** in the lead OWD sharing setting

There are various items that work together to control record visibility and accessibility for each user. They are covered in the following sections.

Record ownership

Each record in Salesforce is owned by a user or queue (queue is only available for Case, Lead, and Custom Object) as long as the object is not configured as a child in a master-detail relationship. By default, the user who creates the record is the record owner, unless you have assignment rules, workflows with field updates, or triggers that change the record owner. The record owner has full access to the record, but they can only edit, share, and delete the record when the owner has the right permissions to read, edit, and delete permissions on that object level permission.

The Organization-Wide Default (OWD) sharing setting

The **Organization-Wide Defaults** (OWD) sharing setting specifies the level of access for users to each object:

- **Private**: Data is visible only to the record owner, users with sharing access, and users in the higher level in the role hierarchy of users who are able to read or edit the record.
- **Public Read-Only**: All users are able to see the data in the object, regardless of the record owner. But, the record is only editable by the record owner, users with read/write sharing access, and users in the higher level in the role hierarchy of users that are able to edit the record.
- **Public Read Write**: All users are able to see and edit all of the data.
- **Controlled by Parent**: This is only for the child object of a master-detail relationship and some standard objects, such as `Contact`. Record visibility for this setting depends on the parent setting.

 A child object of a master-detail relationship will always have access controlled by the parent, and it is not configurable.

Sharing rules

The administrator is able to configure auto-sharing rules based on record ownership or by specific criteria. With sharing rules, a record can be shared with public groups, roles, and subordinates with the following levels of access:

- **Read Only**
- **Read/Write**

This setting is available in the OWD sharing setting.

Role hierarchy

When **Grant Access Using Hierarchies** is enabled, a user in the upper role hierarchy is automatically able to access all of the data owned by their subordinates, no matter what the OWD sharing setting is, but you must ensure that the user has permission for access to the concerned object.

For a standard object, access by users in the higher role hierarchies is enabled by default and cannot be turned off. While for custom objects, it is also enabled by default, but the admin has the ability to disable it.

This setting is also available in the OWD sharing setting.

Object permission

Each object has its own permission setting (both standard and custom objects), including child objects of master-detail relationships. The permissions are as follows:

- **Read**
- **Create**
- **Edit**
- **Delete**
- **View All**, where the user is able to view all records for that object regardless of who the record owner is
- **Modify All**, where the user is able to edit all records for that object regardless of who the record owner is

An object permission is defined in **Profile** or **Permission Set** for specific users.

System permission

A user with the **View All Data** permission is able to access all of the data across an organization for all objects, while a user with the **Modify All Data** permission can modify all of the data across an organization for all objects. This setting is also defined in the **Profile** or **Permission Set** page.

Manual sharing

The record owner, a user in the higher role hierarchy of the record owner, and an administrator are able to manually share data with other users, groups, roles, and subordinates by clicking on the **Sharing** button. Ensure that this button is available on the page layout.

Apex-managed sharing

Apex-managed sharing provides developers with the ability to write apex code or SOAP API code to programmatically share record access to standard or custom objects with a user or group, and determine the access level from among **Read**, **Edit**, and **All**.

Summary

This chapter is primarily intended for Salesforce system administrators, but it is also good for business users to understand more of data management in Salesforce. In this chapter, we started with discussing data backup in Salesforce.com, how to back up, the tools available, and why we need to back up.

We continued to discuss the Salesforce Sandbox environment, type of Sandbox, and usage of each type of Sandbox. Next, you learned how to import data to Salesforce with the help of multiple tools.

At the end of the chapter, we highlighted items that determined user accessibility to a record, from record owner to manual and apex sharing.

The next chapter will be more interesting, as we will start building our very own Salesforce report.

3
Creating Your First Report

This chapter introduces you to practical report creation. Before we go on to report creation, we will discuss permissions related to creating, editing, and deleting reports. Also, other permissions such as exporting a report to Excel or CSV file format will be discussed.

Each report can be stored in a report folder because we need to use it in the future or share it within our team. Therefore, we will discuss permissions related to report folders. From there on, we will continue with the available standard report provided by Salesforce, and the additional user interface available for designing reports. You will also learn how to export a report.

By the end of this chapter, you will have gained the knowledge required to create a simple report using standard report types provided for most standard or custom objects. You will also know how to create a custom report type when the standard report type is not enough.

Throughout this chapter, we will provide notes and tips to help you understand important items. The topics covered in this chapter are:

- Report permissions
- Folder report and folder permissions
- Report types
- Report creation
- Exporting reports
- Additional user interface setup for reports

Report permissions

Before we start to create a report, you must know that there are a few permissions that determine the ability of a user to create, run, export, and schedule reports in Salesforce.

Run Reports

Without the **Run Reports** permission, you will not be able to open any Salesforce report; in Salesforce, open report is the same as run report with the latest data. When you try to click on the **Reports** tab or even type in the report URL, you will get the **Insufficient Privileges** error message.

When all users in a profile need to run a report, the administrator can simply enable this permission in the **Profile** settings in the **General User Permissions** section. To assign this permission to users in different profiles, use the **Permission Set** option. Remember that **Permission Set** is used to give more permissions per user basis, not to remove permissions from the user.

This permission also controls the ability of the user to access dashboards. We will cover dashboards in *Chapter 6, Creating Your First Dashboard*. If you cannot run a report, contact your administrator to get this permission enabled.

You can perform a quick check to find out whether you have this permission enabled. Click on the **Reports** tab, and you should see something similar to what is shown in the following screenshot. But, if the permission is not enabled, you will see the **Insufficient Privileges** error message. If you do not see the **Reports** tab at all, click on the **+** tab to show all the tabs available for you.

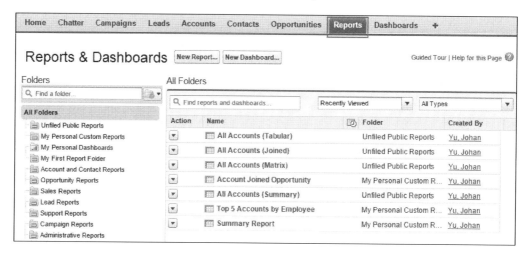

Create and Customize Reports

The permission to create and customize reports controls the user's ability to create new reports or modify existing reports. Without this permission, the user will not see the **New Report…** button when they are in the **Reports** tab. This permission requires the **Run Reports** permission, so if the **Run Reports** permission is disabled for a user, **Create and Customize Reports** is also automatically disabled for that user.

When you have this permission enabled, you should see the **New Report…** button visible, as shown in the following screenshot. Otherwise, it means you do not have permission to create and customize reports. Discuss with your administrator to get this enabled. Users without the **Create and Customize Reports** permission are still able to run reports, but are not able to customize and save them; all the filters will be grayed out.

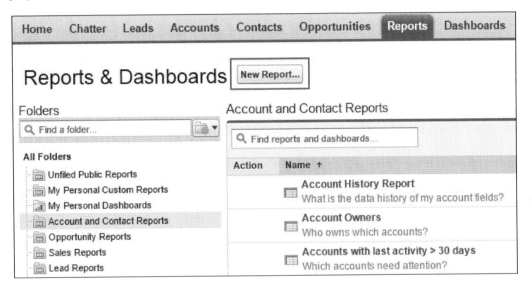

Export Reports

The **Export Reports** permission manages the user's ability to export a report in Excel or CSV file format. Similar to the **Create and Customize Reports** permission, this permission also depends on the **Run Reports** permission. Disabling **Run Reports** will automatically disable this permission.

Users with this permission enabled will see the **Printable View** and **Export Details** buttons when they run a report.

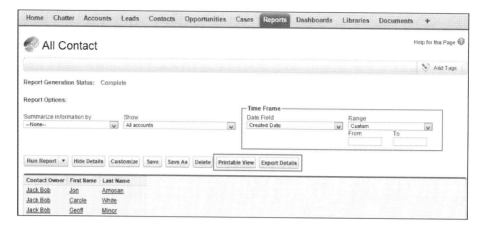

Schedule Reports

The **Schedule Reports** permission enables users to schedule reports for a future run. You can schedule a report frequency as daily, weekly, or monthly, and you also have to set a preferred start time. When the report runs on schedule, an e-mail with the report result will be sent to all the users who have been included in the recipient list for that report. You can specify users, public groups, or roles to be included.

Users without this permission will not see the **Schedule Future Runs...** option in the **Run Report** drop-down menu.

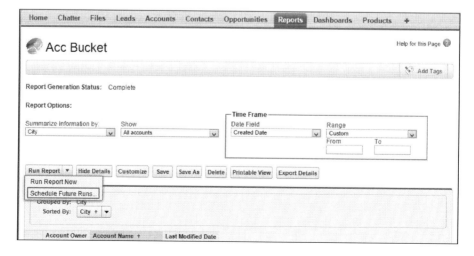

Report Builder

The **Report Builder** permission enables a powerful drag-and-drop editor to replace old report wizards to create and edit reports. If your organization started using Salesforce after 2010, **Report Builder** is activated by default for your organization. Otherwise, you will see an option to enable it for the organization. Navigate to **Setup | Customize | Reports & Dashboards | User Interface**. Once this is enabled, you cannot turn it off.

For system administrators, organization-wide control always supersedes profile control, which means that if organization-wide control of a Report Builder is enabled, all users will use Report Builder, regardless of whether this permission is enabled or not for the user in the profile or permission set.

If you do not have **Report Builder** permissions enabled and it is also not enabled for the whole organization, you will see the **Report Wizard** screen after clicking on the **New Report...** button. **Report Wizard** is an older technology compared to the latest **Report Builder**.

For this book, moving forward, we will only use **Report Builder** rather than the old **Report Wizard**.

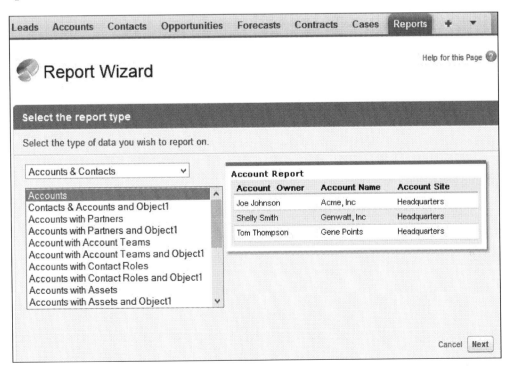

Salesforce report folders

By default, Salesforce comes with a lot of standard reports. They are stored and categorized by the object name and purpose, such as **Account and Contact Reports**, **Opportunity Reports**, and so on. The same applies to report created and customized created by users. Users can store them in folders for future use or other purposes, for example, as a data source for dashboards or sharing with other users. Depending on the user permission and folder permission, Salesforce will determine the folder's visibility and accessibility to a user, as read-only or read-write accessibility. Remember that report accessibility is configured in the folder level, not in the report itself.

 When a folder is visible to a user, the user will be able to see and run all the reports stored in that folder.

When you click on the **Reports** tab, you will see all the report and dashboard folders you have access to in the left panel.

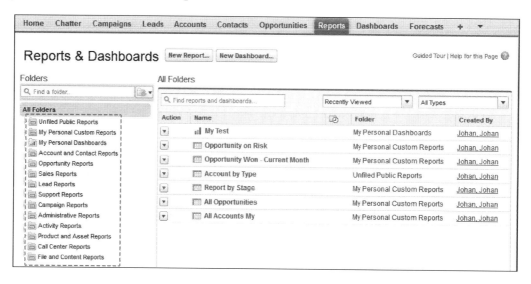

Users with read-write permission on the folder will be able to save reports to that particular folder. Therefore, when you save a report, you will see all report folders that you have write permission to. The **Save Report** dialog box is shown in the following screenshot:

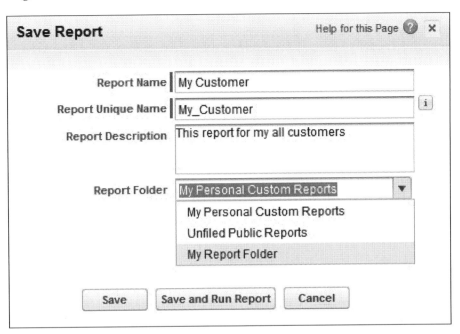

Each folder can store either reports or dashboards, but not both. A common naming pattern is to add a report and dashboard label to the report name; for example, create an `Accounts Reports` folder and an `Accounts Dashboards` folder to help keep things organized. The report folder and dashboard folder are both located in the **Reports** tab, but you can easily differentiate the report and dashboard folders from the different icons before the folder names.

You can imagine the report folder as the Windows Explorer folder, but without the multilevel folder structure. Instead of storing files, the report folder only stores reports.

Report and dashboard folder sharing

Enhanced folder sharing is enabled by default if you've subscribed to Salesforce after Summer 2013 release. If not, your admin can turn on this option. This option will enable access-level sharing for report and dashboard folders.

To activate enhanced folder sharing, navigate to **Setup | Customize | Reports & Dashboards | Folder Sharing**. Tick **Enable access levels for sharing report and dashboard folders** to enable enhanced folder sharing.

When enhanced folder sharing is enabled, you will see the **Share** option when you hover your mouse over the report folder and click on the pin icon next to the folder name.

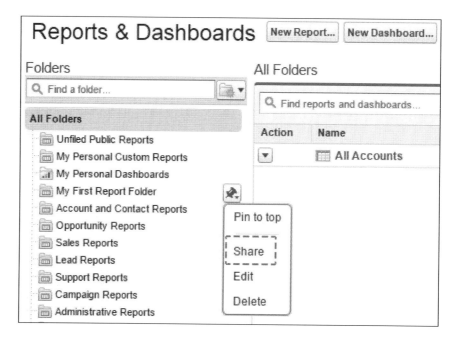

A user can share a report folder with other users, roles, roles and subordinates, or public groups, with the level of access as **Viewer**, **Editor**, and **Manager**.

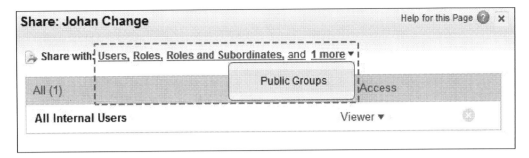

To share a report folder, the user must have either **Manager** access to that report folder or the **Manage Reports in Public Folders** permission.

 When you create a folder, you will be automatically set as **Manager** for that folder.

Enhanced folder sharing offers three levels of access for report and dashboard folders, as shown in the following table:

Viewer	Editor	Manager
• View a folder in the folder tree • View all of the content • Run reports and refresh dashboards	• All access from the **Viewer** access option • Edit all of the content of a folder • Add content to a folder • Delete content from a folder	• All types of access from the **Editor** access option • Edit a folder name • Edit, delete, or remove shares

Hands-on – creating a report folder

We will now create a report folder with the help of the following steps:

1. Navigate to the **Reports** tab.

2. Click on **New Report Folder** under the folder icon.

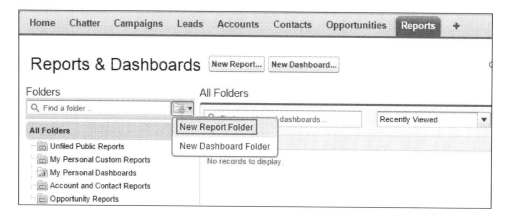

3. Enter `My First Report Folder` in the **Report Folder Label** textbox.

4. Click on the **Save** button.

   The folder created will be shown in the **All Folders** area of the left panel in the **Reports** tab.

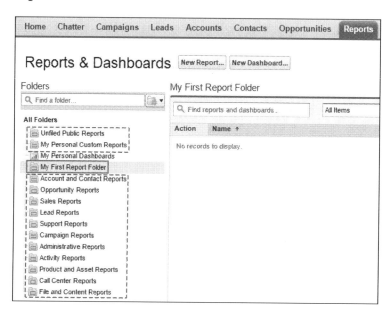

Looking at the preceding screenshot, let's now see what each folder is used for:

- The `Unified Public Reports` folder is a report folder accessible by everyone as long as users have the **Run Reports** permission. If the user has the **Create and Customize Reports** permission, they will be able to save a report in this folder for public sharing.

 Since this folder is accessible by everyone and it can also be edited by anyone, be careful not to store your private or important reports in this folder.

- The `My Personal Custom Reports` folder is a secure folder where you can store your personal reports. No one can access reports inside this folder, not even your system administrator.

- The folders from `Account and Contact Reports` to `File and Content Reports` are standard report folders that come with Salesforce. Users have read-only access to these folders, which means that users are able to run reports, but not able to save reports in these folders.

 The system admin may hide these folders from users if they are not applicable for the organization.

Hands-on – sharing a report folder

You will now understand the steps involved in sharing a report folder.

Suppose we want to share `My First Report Folder` with users in the CEO role as viewers, and the assistant is named Novida Lunardi, who is able to modify reports in this folder, and to share the report folder to other users. Assume that the role of the CEO has been created and a user named Novida Lunardi has also been created:

1. Navigate to the **Reports** tab.

2. Click on the **My First Report Folder** report folder created earlier, hover your mouse over a report name, click on the pin icon, and then click on the **Share** link.

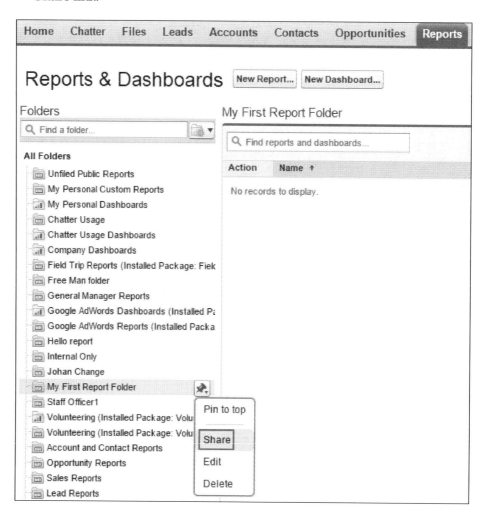

3. This will open a pop-up window. Click on the **Roles** link and then on the **Shared** button next to **CEO**. Leave the access menu as **Viewer** and click on the **Done** button to continue.

4. Next, click on the **Users** link, look for **Novida Lunardi**, and click on the **Shared** button next to that user. The default access is **Viewer**. Click on the arrow next to it and select **Manager**. Then click on the **Done** button to continue.

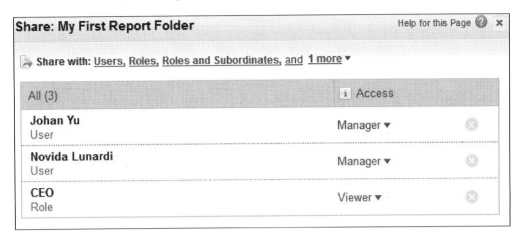

5. Click on the **Close** button to close the window.

In this exercise, you learned how to share a report folder with a user with `Manager` access and users in a role that allows them to view reports.

Folder permissions

When **Enhanced Folder Sharing** is disabled, there is only one permission available related to the report folder—**Manage Public Reports**. Once this is enabled, you will see it leading to:

- **Create Report Folders**
- **Edit My Reports**
- **Manage Reports in Public Folders**
- **View Reports in Public Folders**

Manage Public Reports

Run Reports and **Create and Customize Reports** permissions are required to enable the **Manage Public Reports** permission. When this permission is enabled from **Profile** or **Permission Set**, users are able to create a new report folder and edit the report folder visible to them. However, only users with the **View All Data** permission can see and edit all public folders.

Create Report Folders

The **Create Report Folders** permission gives users the ability to create new report folders. The **Create and Customize Reports** permission is required to enable this permission. When this permission is enabled, once you click on the **Reports** tab, you will see a folder icon next to the **All Folders** area. Once you click on the folder icon, you can select the **New Report Folder** menu. Now you just need to provide a label in **Report Folder Label** to create the folder.

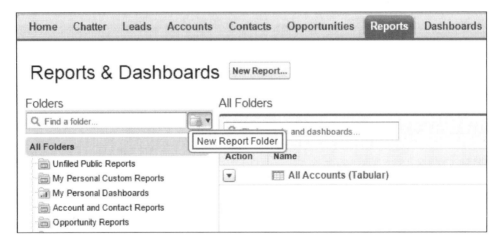

Edit My Reports

The **Edit My Reports** permission allows users to edit, move, save, and delete reports created by them in shared folders. If a user with this permission has access to a report folder, they will be able to save reports in this report folder. Even user accessibility to the report folder can only be set as **Viewer**. The user is also able to edit and delete reports created by them in a public report folder where they have **Viewer** access.

Without this permission, when user accessibility to the report folder is **Viewer**, the user will not be able to overwrite reports stored in the `Public` folder even if the report is created by that user.

This permission is not supposed to be given to everyone. It allows users to store reports in any public report folder that they have access to, even with **Viewer** access.

View Reports in Public Folders

The **View Reports in Public Folders** permission gives the user visibility and access to all public report folders, although the user is not listed in the sharing access for that particular report folder. As in the case of the **Edit My Reports** permission, this permission is also not supposed to be given to normal end users.

Manage Reports in Public Folders

The **Manage Reports in Public Folders** permission requires the **View Reports in Public Folders**, **Edit My Reports**, and **Create Report Folders** permission rights to be enabled. With this permission, users are able to access and edit all reports in the `Public` report folder.

Additionally, this permission allows users to share, edit, and delete any public report folder, so it is a very powerful permission.

Be careful to give this permission only to those users who absolutely need it; ensure that users with this permission will not mess up important reports created by other users.

Now that you have an idea of all the permissions that are related to the report folder and which are required for some users, let's move on to the **Report Builder** tool and the various types of reports that can be created.

Report Builder

Early in this chapter, we discussed the **Report Builder** permission, but **Report Builder** itself is a tool used to create and customize reports to replace the older **Report Wizard**. **Report Builder** offers the intuitive drag-and-drop method to create new reports and customize existing reports easily in one screen with point-and-click and no coding.

The components available in **Report Builder** may be slightly different, depending on the primary object used in the report type; for example, a case report will have the **Units** option in minutes, hours, and days, while an opportunity report will have filters for **Status** and **Probability**.

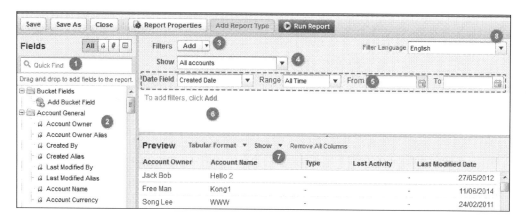

Looking at the preceding screenshot for the standard account report type, let's now cover the components available in **Report Builder**:

- You can type field names in the **Quick Find** section (**1**) to quickly find a field available for reports. Once you've typed in this textbox, only fields matching the text will be displayed.

- All fields available for a particular report type will be shown in the **Fields** section (**2**).

- You can add **Field Filter**, **Filter Logic**, **Cross Filter**, and **Row Limit** from the **Filters** option (**3**).

- The value in the **Show** pick list (**4**) depends on the report type used. For an opportunity report, you will find the **My team's opportunities** option. This option is used to show all opportunities owned by you and your team.

- In the **Date Field** section (**5**), you can add filters to reports based on any date field available for the report type used.

- You can drag and drop fields into the filter area (**6**) for filtering. This area will also show any filter added for the report.

- In the **Preview** panel **(7)**, you will find an option to select the report format, an option to show details, a currency option, and a link to remove all selected fields for the report. You also can drag and drop fields into this area. A field added will show a red cross when you drag it into the report area, not all data will be shown in the preview window.

- In the **Filter Language** section **(8)**, if you have **Translation Workbench** enabled, you can filter translated strings by specifying the language.

We will go through each of the preceding components in the last topic of this chapter when we start creating reports.

Standard reports and folders

Out of the box, Salesforce provides standard reports for standard objects. These reports are stored in standard report folders:

- `Account and Contact Reports`
- `Opportunity Reports`
- `Sales Reports`
- `Lead Reports`
- `Support Reports`: for `Cases`
- `Campaign Reports`
- `Activity Reports`: for `Tasks` and `Events`
- `Product and Asset Reports`
- `Call Center Reports`
- `Administrative Reports`: for system administrators
- `File and Content Reports`

You can customize standard reports provided by Salesforce, but you have to save them as a new report so that we do not overwrite the originals. Also, you cannot save the customized report in the standard report folder, but only in the `Public` report folder — where you have write access — or the `My Personal Custom Reports` folder.

Report types

Every Salesforce report, including standard reports and custom reports, is built on a report type. A report type defines the set of records and fields available for a report based on the relationships between a primary object and the related objects defined.

 To report data from a custom object, make sure you enable **Allow Reports** for that object.

Ideally, report type creation and maintenance is under the job scope of Salesforce administrators, not business users.

When a custom object is enabled for a report, Salesforce will automatically create a report type, with the report type name being the same as the plural name of the object. This report type is stored in the `Other Reports` category folder.

For example, let's say we have a custom object called `Expense`, **Enable Reports** and **Track Field History** has been enabled for this object.

When you go to the **Reports** tab and create a new report, you will find a few report types automatically created for you.

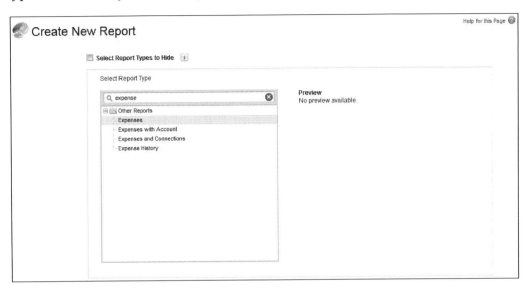

Typing expense in the search textbox will produce four report types available for use:

- **Expenses**: This report type will contain all fields related to the Expense object.

- **Expenses with Account**: This report type is created because we have a lookup field for Account in the Expense object.

- **Expenses and Connections**: This report type is created because we configured Salesforce to Salesforce in this organization.

- **Expense History**: This report type is created as we activate **Track Field History**, as shown in one of the preceding screenshots.

Report type category

A report type category is stored in folders, which makes it easier to find the right report type when you are creating a new report. Depending on your Salesforce edition, you may get different report type categories.

You cannot create a new report type category, but you can create a custom report type and store it in one of the categories provided. It is always good practice to store the custom report type in the right category.

Over the years, you may have too many report types created, but many of them are seldom used or used only once. As an administrator, you can hide those report types from user selection when creating new reports.

When you create a new report, click on **Select Report Types to Hide** and then on the report type name to hide it. The icon will change from a tick to a cross.

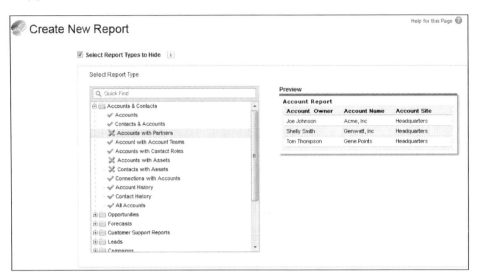

Click on **Select Report Types to Hide** again to hide the selection option. All the report types hidden will no longer be available for use.

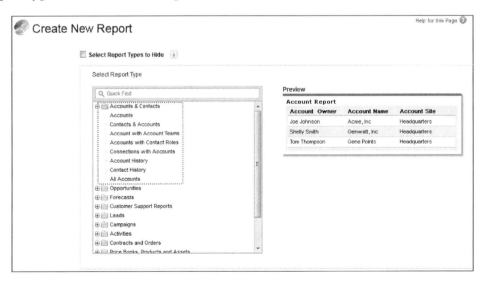

The structure of a report type category is a little similar to the standard report folder, but do not get confused between the two. The standard report folder contains standard reports provided by Salesforce out of the box. You will not be able to overwrite them, but you can modify and save the reports as new reports in a custom public report folder or your personal report folder.

The report type category stores all types of reports, including standard and custom report types. You can store custom report types in any report type category, but you cannot create or add a new report type category.

Standard report types

When you click on the **New Report...** button from the **Reports** tab, you will be presented with a list of report type categories.

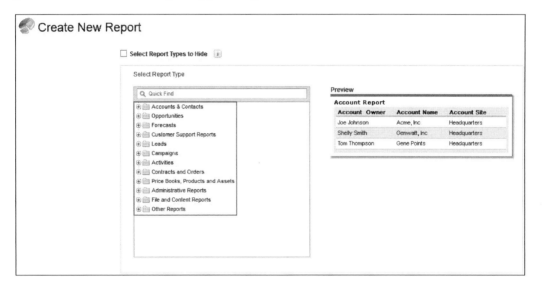

There are two types of standard report types:

- The report type that comes with Salesforce for standard objects, such as **Contacts & Accounts**. You can easily recognize this report type, as it will have a **Preview** section when you select that report type when creating a new report.

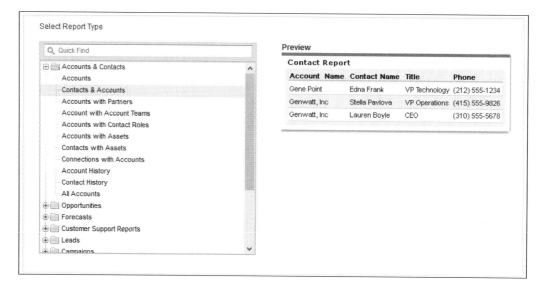

- The report type that is autogenerated by Salesforce when you enable the **Allow Report** option for custom objects. This report type will not have **Preview**; it will just say **No preview available**.

When you relate an object to another object and both objects are enabled for reports, the following options will occur, depending on the lookup relationship. In the following example, we will use Customer as the parent object and Claim as the child object.

Let's look closer at both the relationships to know what will happen with the report type once the relationship for those objects is built:

- **Lookup relationship**: The following process is performed in the lookup relationship:

    ○ When we activate **Enable Reports** for the `Claim` object, Salesforce will automatically create the `Claims` report type. When we relate `Claims` to the `Customers` object as a lookup relationship, Salesforce will automatically add the `Customer` field to the `Claims` report type. Users will see an additional field named `Customer`, but no other fields from the `Customer` object will be available for the report.

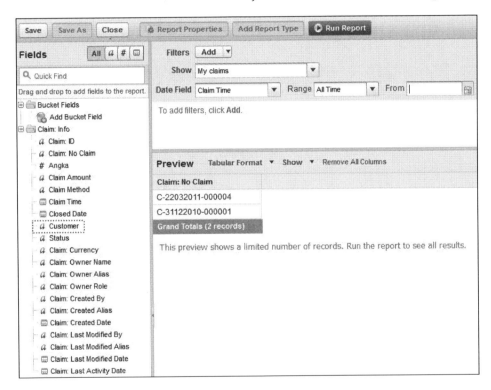

○ There is no change in the existing `Customers` report type because `Customer` is the parent object.

○ A new report type called `Claims with Customer` will be created in the `Other Reports` category folder. This report type will contain all the fields available for both the `Claim` and `Customer` objects, but will only show the `Claims with Customer` records. This means the `Claims` record without `Customer` will not be in the report generated.

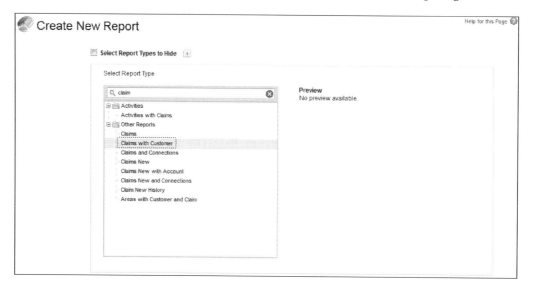

• **Master-detail relationship**: The following process is performed in the master-detail relationship:

○ When we activate **Enable Reports** for the `Claim` object, Salesforce will automatically create the `Claims` report type. When we relate `Claim` to the `Customer` object as a child in the master-detail relationship, the existing `Claims` report type will no longer be available because it became a child of the `Customer` object in a master-detail relationship.

○ There is no change in the existing `Customers` report type because `Customer` is the parent object.

○ A new report type called `Customers with Claims` will be created in the `Other Reports` category folder. Notice the difference between this report type and the report type automatically created in the lookup relationship. This report has all the fields available from both `Customer` and `Claim` objects and will show `Customer` with `Claim` only. This means the `Customer` object without `Claim` will not be in the report generated.

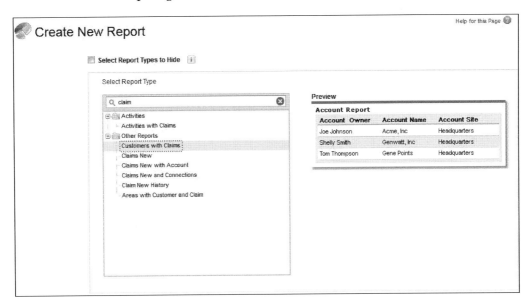

Custom report types

A report type defines the set of records and fields available for a report. The source of the report type can only be from an object, or include related objects. The report type also determines the records displayed in the report that meet the criteria defined in it.

When standard report types do not meet the reporting requirements, your administrator can create custom report types. Custom report types support multi-level object relationships, define parent-level objects as primary objects, and relate down to the child object and grandchild object—not the other way round.

For example, let's say you have an object relationship of Customer with child Claim, and Claim with child Claim Payment. In this relationship, you can build a custom report type, **Customer with Claim and Claim Payment**, but not **Claim Payment with Claim and Customer**.

Using the `Customer` and `Claim` objects that we discussed in the *Standard report types* section, in a master-detail relationship, customers with claims will be automatically created.

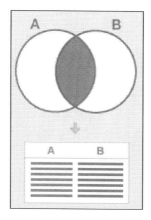

In the preceding figure, **A** is `Customer` and **B** is `Claim`. The `Customers with Claims` standard report type is autogenerated by Salesforce. When you relate the objects, Salesforce will generate a report of customers with claims only; customers without claims will not be available in the report. You can generate a report using the `Customers` report type to produce all customers, but it will have no claim information in that report type.

In this scenario, a custom report type comes into the picture. We can create a custom report type, `Customers`, with or without `Claims`. This report type will generate customer information with claim information, including customers that do not have any claims. The following diagram displays the scenario, where **A** stands for Customer and **B** for Claim:

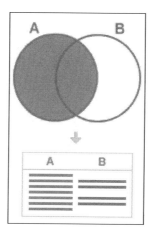

With a custom report type, we can define a primary object and relate it to the child objects. There are two options when you relate a parent to a child object in report types:

- A record in the primary object must have at least one record of the related object, otherwise the parent record will not be shown in the report

- A record in the primary object may or may not have records of related objects

With a custom report type, you can define which objects' fields can be used as columns in reports. If a field is removed from a custom report type, a particular field in all reports built on that report type will be automatically removed.

Hands-on – create a custom report type

Only users with the **Manage Custom Report Types** permission are able to create custom report types. For this exercise, we will create a new custom report type where Customer is the primary object. It may or may not have Claim, and Claim may or may not have Claim Payment. Assume that all objects have been created and enabled for the report:

1. Navigate to **Setup | Create | Report Types**, and click on the **New Custom Report Type** button.

2. In the **Primary Object** section, select objects that will be in the top hierarchy for the report type. In this exercise, select **Customers**.

Once the record type is saved, you cannot change the primary object in the future.

3. Enter the **Report Type Label** and the **Report Type Name** values. The label can be up to 255 characters long. For this exercise, label it as Customers with/without Claims with/without Claim Payments. The name will be automatically populated. You can modify it, but just leave it as it is for this exercise.

4. Enter the **Description** data for the custom report type. You can enter up to 1,000 characters. This description is mandatory and will be shown when users select the report type to create a report. Provide a meaningful description so that users get a good idea of which data is available for reports, for example, All customers with Claim information.

5. Select **Store in Category**. Always store a report type in the correct category for users to find the report type easily. Select **Other Reports**.

6. Select **Deployment Status** and click on the **Next** button to continue. There are two options:

    ○ **In Development**: The report type with this status will only be available for users with the **Manage Custom Report Types** permission. Select this option during the design and testing phases. The report type and its reports are hidden from all other users.

    ○ **Deployed**: The report type and its report will be available for everyone. Change the deployment status to this option after the report is tested and is ready to let all users access it.

7. Click on the **Next** button to continue.

8. Customers will be shown as the primary object. Click on **(click to relate to another object)** to relate to the child object. For our exercise, select **Claims**. Then do the same to relate **Claims** to **Claim Payments**.

9. Click on the **Save** button to finish.

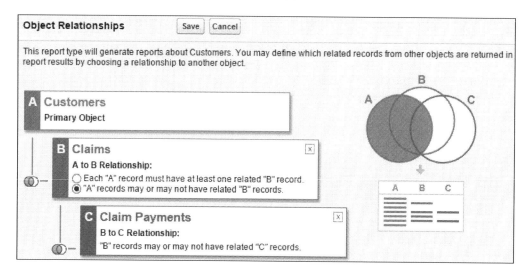

Custom report types start from top-level objects as primary objects and support only one child object in the same level, but allow you to build multiple levels of parent and child hierarchies.

You can use **Add fields related via lookup** to get the parent object's fields to the report type from the **Edit Layout** button. You do not need to define the parent object in the object relationship.

Creating your first report

We have discussed many topics in this chapter related to creating a report, which include:

- Report permissions
- Report folders
- Folder permissions
- Report components
- Standard reports
- Report types

Well, let's start creating a simple, custom report, and from now onwards, we'll just call a custom report as report.

Hands-on – creating a report

The necessary steps involved in creating a report are as follows:

1. Navigate to the **Reports** tab.

If you don't see the **Reports** tab, click on the + icon in the last tab to show all available tabs. If you still cannot find it, contact your system administrator.

2. You will see the report and dashboard folders in the left panel and the recently viewed reports and dashboards in the main area.

3. Click on the **New Report...** button.

4. Click on **+** in the **Accounts & Contacts** report type category.

5. Select **Accounts**.

6. Click on the **Create** button in the bottom-right corner.

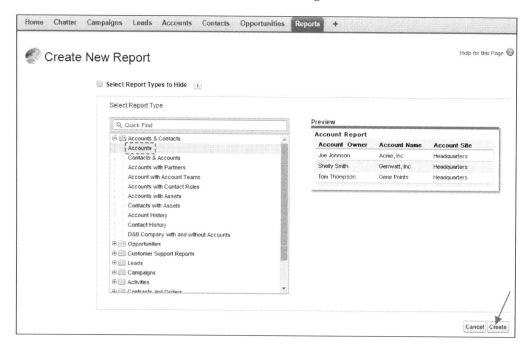

7. By default, it will show **My accounts** with the created date as the present day.

8. If you have not created an account today, nothing will be shown in the report preview. You can change the **Range** filter from **Custom** to **All Time** to see a report of all the accounts owned by you.

9. Click on the **Run Report** button. Before you run the report, it will show limited number of records, which are only for a preview. You have to click on **Run Report** to get entire records.

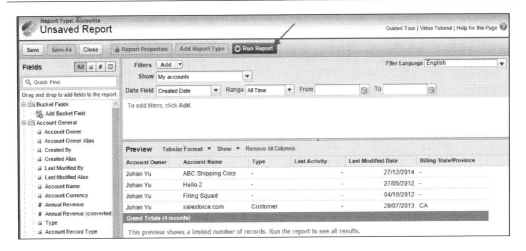

You have successfully created your very own first record. Congrats!

10. Click on the **Save** button to save the report for future use or to share with your team. Notice that the **Save As** button is greyed because you create the report from scratch, rather than modifying an existing report.

11. Enter the report name and report description and select a report folder. You will see all the folders where you have access as **Editor** or **Manager**.

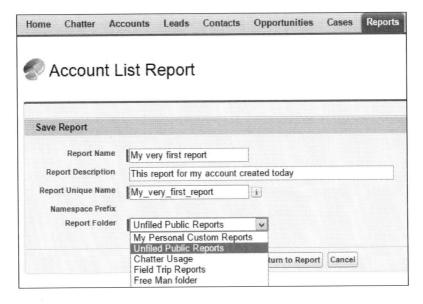

12. For this exercise, select the **Unfiled Public Reports** folder. This folder is accessible by all users in your organization with the **Create and Customize Reports** permission. As far as reports that other users don't need to see are concerned, you can save them in your private report folder called `My Personal Custom Reports`. This will ensure that no one can access and change the report.

13. Click on the **Save** button to return to the **Reports** tab, or click on **Save & Return to Report** to get back to the report again. For this exercise, just click on the **Save** button.

14. You will notice **My very first report** appear at the top of the list of reports, because this is the most recent report you view or work on. The report description will be shown below the report name.

15. Click on the report again to open the report. When you open a report, it will be automatically refreshed with the latest available data.

16. Notice that nothing has changed since you saved the report, be it columns, report criteria, time frame, or anything else.

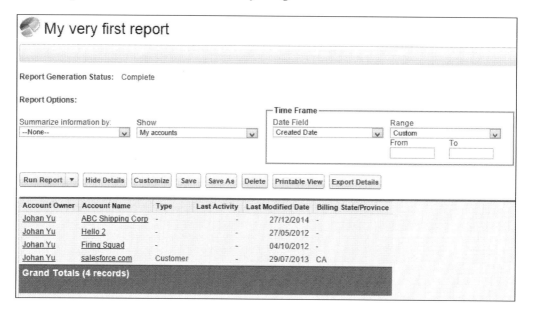

Exporting a report

Once a report is generated in Salesforce, if you have the **Export Reports** permission, you will be able to export the report's details to an Excel file or CSV file. There are two ways to export reports:

1. Navigate to the **Reports** tab.
2. Open a report by clicking on the report name.
3. Click on the **Printable View** button or **Export Details** button.

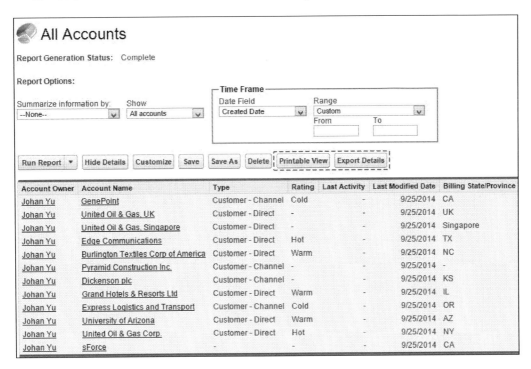

You can also directly export reports from the **Reports** tab. Click on the arrow before the report name and then select **Export**.

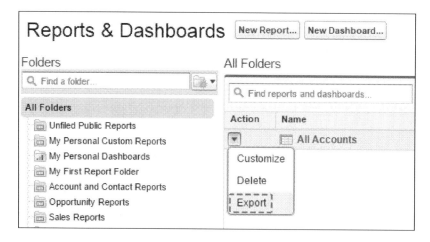

Export and **Export Details** will produce the same file format. The user has the option to save the file in Excel or CSV format, while **Printable View** always returns the file in Excel format.

The file generated from **Export Details** will be in the raw format, while **Printable View** will maintain the report format in the Excel file, including:

- Report name
- Report generator and timestamp
- Report filter
- Sorting
- Grouping and field count
- Fields summary

Additional report user interface setup

The system administrator or users with the **Customize Application** permission are able to enable or disable additional settings related to the report. These features may help users to get more out of the reports option. They may be related to the reports' user interface and the reports generated. These settings are applied to all reports generated or exported to the file, but they do not affect the data returned in the reports and dashboards.

Enable Floating Report Headers

Navigate to **Setup | Customize | Reports & Dashboards | User Interface** to enable or disable the **Enable Floating Report Headers** option.

Report and Dashboard User Interface Settings

Modify the behavior of the user interface for report and dashboard pages using the following settings:

User Interface

☑ Enable Floating Report Headers
☑ Export Reports Without Footers ⓘ
☐ Enable Dashboard Finder ⓘ

Chatter Options

☐ Enable Dashboard Component Snapshots ⓘ

When the **Enable Floating Report Headers** option is enabled, a report header will be floating and always visible, no matter how far you scroll down in the report. Once you scroll below the first row, you will see a small triangle icon. It will hide the header when you click on it. When the header is not shown, clicking on this icon will bring the header back into view, as shown in the following screenshot:

Account Owner	Account Name	Type	Last Activity	Last Modified Date
Song Lee	WWW		-	24/02/2011
Maria Ann	TestH	-	-	24/02/2011
Maria Ann	Star Disc	Analyst	03/04/2013	15/03/2013
Free Man	Ahui Jack	-	-	13/10/2014
Linda Yie	Ahui Song	-	-	14/08/2014
Free Man	Ahui Maria	-	23/01/2012	13/08/2014
Jack Bob	1	-	-	11/05/2014

Export Reports Without Footers

The **Export Reports Without Footers** option is located at the same place as **Enable Floating Report Headers**. When this option is enabled, report exported to an Excel or CSV file will not have report information at the bottom of the file. We've discussed **Export Reports** in previous topics in this chapter.

If your Salesforce organization does not enable **Enable Floating Report Headers**, you will see a report footer at the bottom of the report, like this:

All Accounts Report

Copyright (c) 2000-2014 salesforce.com, inc. All rights reserved.

Confidential Information - Do Not Distribute

Generated By: Johan Yu 03/11/2014 06:27

SimplySfdc

[This option is related only to **Export Details**, not **Printable View**.]

Summary

In this chapter, we thoroughly discussed the components related to report creation. We started with the types of permissions related to reports. Users without appropriate report permissions will not be able to perform some activities; for example, not everyone is allowed to export reports. The same applies to other permissions. They are assigned via profiles or using permission sets to assign permissions for specific users.

We continued with the report folder, where each report is stored in a report folder. With folder sharing, we can determine which users are able to access which report folder. Just allow **Run Reports** or even modify existing reports.

We discussed multiple components in **Report Builder**, continuing with report types, which determine records and fields available in the report generated. When the standard report type is not able to generate reports as required, we can create custom report types with specific fields and data sources.

At the end of the chapter, we created a new simple report, and you learned how to export it in multiple types of files.

In the next chapter, we will go deeper into working with reports, starting with the report format, managing custom report types, and adding a chart to a report.

4

Working with Reports

You learned about many components related to reports in *Chapter 3, Creating Your First Report,* starting with report folders, permissions related to reports and report folders, report types, creating a new report from scratch, and how to export reports as CSV or Excel files.

In this chapter, we will continue to discuss working with reports. We will cover multiple types of report formats, working with report filters, managing custom report types, adding charts to reports, and subscribing to reports.

By end of this chapter, you will gain knowledge on selecting a report format based on the requirements, and understand how to customize it using report filters. You also will gain advanced knowledge on custom report types and adding charts to reports. As a business user, you can fully utilize subscribe report to be alert if something goes wrong.

Throughout this chapter, we will provide notes and tips to help you understand important items. The topics covered in this chapter are as follows:

- Selecting a report format
- Adding a chart to a report
- Working with report filters
- Managing custom report types
- Subscribing to a report

Selecting the report format

Each Salesforce report is constructed with a report format. The report format will determine the report layout, options, and settings for the report.

There are a few types of report formats in Salesforce, from the simplest tabular report to the complex matrix and joined reports. Each report format has a different usage and purpose.

Choosing a report format

When you create a new report, tabular is the default report format selected. You will be able to modify the report format anytime, even after you save the report, but you may lose some of the settings, depending on the original and target report formats.

There are four report formats available:

- Tabular
- Summary
- Matrix
- Joined

Let's understand them individually.

Tabular report format

The tabular report is the default report format when you create a new report. This format is considered the simplest; it presents data in a manner similar to that of a spreadsheet. Data will be present in the row-and-column format. Each row represents one record and each column represents one Salesforce field; the available fields depend on the report type used. We discussed report types in *Chapter 3, Creating Your First Report*. A report type determines fields available for the report, and it may have all or some fields from one object or related objects.

Although it is the simplest format, the tabular format offers you the ability to sort data by columns, add filters, add summarize fields, use the field bucket, count the number of records, use the cross filter, and export reports. All of these actions are also possible for summary and matrix reports. The main focus of the tabular report is to let you see the details of each record that meets your filter criteria.

These are the limitations of the tabular format:

- No grouping
- No chart
- Not as data source for dashboards, unless the **Row Limit** filter is added and the dashboard settings configured

This format has the best performance figures when generating reports. The following screenshot shows an example of a tabular report:

Account Owner	Account Name ↑	Type	Last Modified Date	Employees
Johan Yu	Burlington Textiles Corp of America	Customer - Direct	9/25/2014	9,000
John Smith	Dickenson plc	Customer - Channel	11/10/2014	120
Johan Yu	Edge Communications	Customer - Direct	9/25/2014	1,000
Johan Yu	Express Logistics and Transport	Customer - Channel	9/25/2014	12,300
Johan Yu	GenePoint	Customer - Channel	9/25/2014	265
Johan Yu	Grand Hotels & Resorts Ltd	Customer - Direct	9/25/2014	5,600
Johan Yu	Pyramid Construction Inc.	Customer - Channel	9/25/2014	2,680
John Smith	sForce	Prospect	11/10/2014	500
Johan Yu	United Oil & Gas, Singapore	Customer - Direct	9/25/2014	3,000
Johan Yu	United Oil & Gas, UK	Customer - Direct	9/25/2014	24,000
Johan Yu	United Oil & Gas Corp.	Customer - Direct	9/25/2014	145,000
Johan Yu	University of Arizona	Customer - Direct	9/25/2014	39,000
Grand Totals (12 records)				
				242,465

Hands-on – creating a tabular report

Our use case is about showing the first five accounts with information of number of employees from all account, orders by the number of employees in descending order, and only for account with types containing **Customer**. In this exercise, we assume you have more than five accounts with type as Customer:

1. Navigate to the **Reports** tab and click on the **New Report…** button.
2. Select the **Accounts** report type; it is under the **Accounts & Contacts** category.
3. Click on the **Create** button to continue.
4. Change **Show** to **All accounts**.

5. Change the **Date Field** range value to **All Time**:

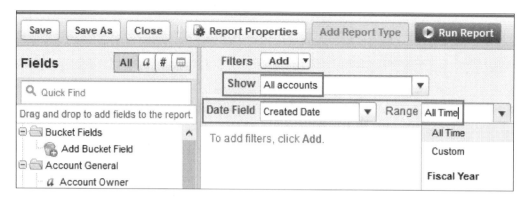

6. Add the **Employees** field to the report area and remove the unnecessary fields, such as **Last Modified Date** and **Rating**.

> You can double-click on the field to add it to the report. If the field has not been added to the report, it will be added to the last column.
>
> You can also drag and drop the field into the report area. Notice the green and red icons when you drag the field. To remove a field from the report, drag the field header and drop it into the field area in the left panel.

7. Click on the **Add** button under **Filters**, and select **Type** from the list of available fields. Select **contains** from the list of operators. Then click on the magnifying glass and select **Customer** from the pop-up list of available type choices. Click on the **OK** button.

8. Click on the small arrow next to the **Add** button, then select **Row Limit** as **5**, sort by **Employees** with the **Descending** order, and click on the **OK** button to apply, as shown in the following screenshot:

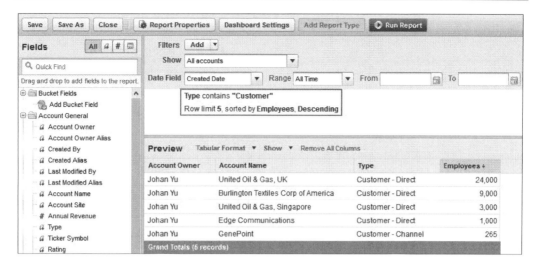

9. Click on the **Run Report** button to see the report results. If everything looks good, click on the **Save As** button. Enter the report name as Top 5 Customers by No of Employee and select **My Personal Custom Reports** in the **Report** Folder.

The summary report format

The main difference between a summary report and a tabular report is the ability to group using any field available for the report. If you do not add any fields for grouping in a summary report, it will run as a tabular report.

A summary report is considered more advanced than a tabular report. In addition to the features stated for the tabular format, a summary report has abilities such as these:

*   Group reports, which are used to group reports based on the values. You can group reports for up to three levels of grouping. You can also summarize data for numeric fields and display record counts for each group.

*   Add a chart to the report.

*   Use the report as the data source for the dashboard. For the tabular report, only the one with the row limit and dashboard settings.

*   Sort by different fields for a group.

*   Ability to hide individual record details to make it easier to see summarized data.

Compared to a tabular report, you cannot add a row limit to a summary format report.

	Employees
Account Owner: John Smith (2 records)	
	620
Type: Customer - Channel (1 record)	
	120
Last Modified Date: CY2014 (1 record)	
	120
Type: Prospect (1 record)	
	500
Last Modified Date: CY2014 (1 record)	
	500
Account Owner: Johan Yu (10 records)	
	241,845
Type: Customer - Channel (3 records)	
	15,245
Last Modified Date: CY2014 (3 records)	
	15,245
Type: Customer - Direct (7 records)	
	226,600
Last Modified Date: CY2014 (7 records)	
	226,600
Grand Totals (12 records)	
	242,465

Hands-on – creating a summary report

Let's cover the following use case: showing all account groups by calendar year of account creation date, and then group by account owner. You need to perform the following steps:

1. Navigate to the **Reports** tab and click on the **New Report...** button.
2. Select the **Accounts** report type. It is under the **Accounts & Contacts** category.
3. Click on the **Create** button to continue.
4. Change **Show** to **All accounts**.
5. Change the **Date Field** range to **All Time**.

6. Change the report format from **Tabular** to **Summary**:

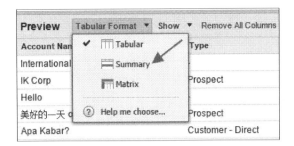

7. Drag **Created Date** into the drop zones in the report. If you do not see the drop zones, enable them by navigating to **Show | Drop Zones**.

 You can type the field name in the textbox fields to filter by field name. If you do not see the grouping zone, click on **Show** and select **Drop Zones**.

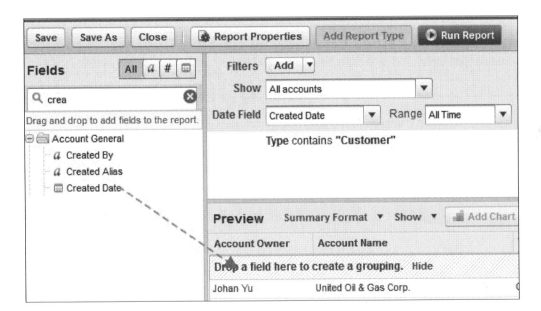

8. Once a field is added to the grouping, click on the arrow to the left of the **Created Date** field, and navigate to **Group Dates By | Calendar Year**, as shown in the following screenshot. **Group Dates By** is only enabled when you group by the date and date/time fields.

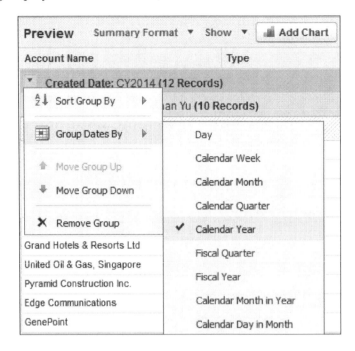

9. Drag **Account Owner** into the drop zones below **Created Date**.

10. By default, the **Details** option will be enabled. Let's disable it for now. Click on the **Show** menu and uncheck **Details**:

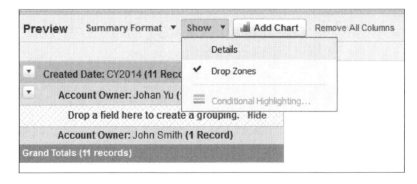

11. Click on **Run Report**. If you have some accounts created in your organization, you should see the sum, as shown in the following screenshot:

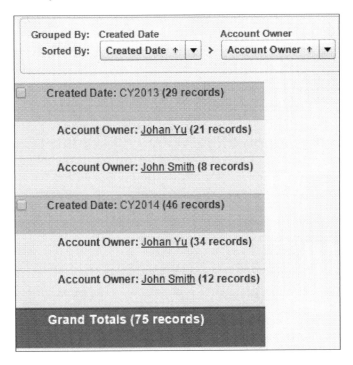

12. By default, the summary report will sort by the first group in ascending order, and then by the second group in ascending order. In our scenario, it is **Created Date**, and then **Account Owner**. You can change the ascending order to descending order by clicking on the respective button in **Sorted By**. You are also able to change the order by the field name or use the record count for each group.

13. Click on the **Show Details** button to show the entire data, but it still is in the same grouping.

14. Click on the **Save** button:

    ○ Report Name = All Account by CY and Owner
    ○ Report Description = All Accounts group by CY and Owner in Summary format
    ○ Report Folder = My Personal Custom Reports

The matrix report format

A matrix report is similar to a summary report, but with the additional capability to group by both rows and columns. You can have up to two levels of grouping for both rows and columns.

Just as in a summary report, in a matrix report, you can add summarizable fields to the matrix. By default, the record count will be added to the report matrix. Once you add some other summary field, you will be able to remove the record count from the report if you don't want it.

This report's format is good when you have a large amount of data to summarize and need to compare records with different values in the same field. Matrix reports without at least one row and one column grouping will be shown as summary reports when you run them.

In this example, the matrix report is showing the same data as the preceding summary report—it's just in a different format:

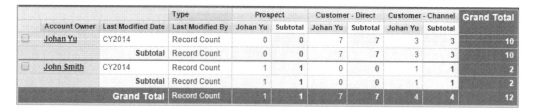

Hands-on – creating a matrix report

Here's our next use case: showing the record count for all accounts in the matrix format, row grouping by calendar year of account creation, and column grouping by account owner. You need to perform the following steps:

1. Navigate to the **Reports** tab and click on the **New Report...** button.
2. Select the **Accounts** report type. It is under the **Accounts & Contacts** category.
3. Click on the **Create** button to continue.
4. Change **Show** to **All Accounts**.
5. Change the **Date Field** range to **All Time**.
6. Change the report format from **Tabular** to **Matrix**.

7. Search for **Created Date** and drag it into the row drop zone:

8. Once **Created Date** is added to the grouping, click on the arrow to the left of the **Created Date** field, and navigate to **Group Dates By | Calendar Year**:

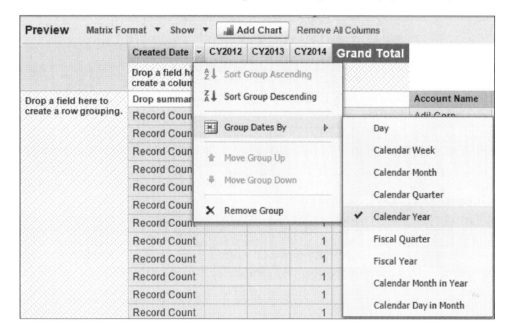

9. Drag **Account Owner** into the column drop zone.

10. By default, **Details** will be enabled. Let's disable it for now. Click on the **Show** menu and uncheck **Details**.

11. Click on **Run Report**. If you have a few accounts created in your organization, you should see something similar to what is shown in the following screenshot:

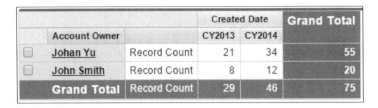

	Account Owner		Created Date		Grand Total
			CY2013	CY2014	
☐	Johan Yu	Record Count	21	34	55
☐	John Smith	Record Count	8	12	20
	Grand Total	Record Count	29	46	75

12. Click on the **Show Details** button to show the data to the right of the matrix.

13. Click on the **Save As** button:

   ○ Report Name = All Account by CY and Owner (Matrix)

   ○ Report Description = All Accounts group by CY and Owner in Matrix format

   ○ Report Folder = My Personal Custom Reports

If you change a report from the summary format to the matrix format:

- A first-level grouping will automatically become a first-level row grouping

- A second-level grouping will automatically become a first-level column grouping

- A third-level grouping will automatically become a second-level row grouping

Joined report format

Joined reports let you create a single report with different types of information. You can get the data from multiple report types and group it by the common fields. Each report in a joined report is displayed in its own report block. The report is presented in multiple blocks, where each block may have the same or different report types.

You can group the report using the common fields. A list of common fields will be shown on top of the **Fields** panel once you have more than one report type in the report. When you customize the joined report, it marks the common fields with a black square icon. The same with matrix and summary reports; you can add summarizable fields to the report's block, and you also can hide the report details to show the reports in a summary.

The filter criteria in a report's blocks are not related to other report blocks, and you cannot relate them. So, make sure to verify that each of them have the right filter. In terms of performance, the more blocks you have, the more the time needed to run a joined report.

	OPPORTUNITIES Won Opportunities		CASES All Cases
	Record Count	Amount	Record Count
Account Name: ABC Song	1	USD 800.00	
Account Name: Acc General	1	USD 35,000.00	1
Account Name: Acme Corp	2	USD 19,002.00	3
Account Name: Ahui Jack	1	USD 71,000.00	
Account Name: Ahui Maria			2
Account Name: Ahui Song	1	USD 40.00	1
Account Name: Big Corp	1	USD 750.00	2
Account Name: Firing Air	1	USD 11,000.00	1
Account Name: Gajah	1	USD 5,000.00	
Account Name: Global Data	1	USD 500,000.00	3
Account Name: Kisaran Corp	2	USD 205,500.00	1
Account Name: New Water Ltd	1	USD 250.00	
Account Name: Star Mart	2	USD 100,180.00	1
Account Name: XYZ Corp			1
Grand Totals	15	USD 948,522.00	16

Hands-on – creating a joined report

Our use case is about showing all the opportunities won and cases related to accounts in one report for the previous year. You need to perform the following steps:

1. Navigate to the **Reports** tab and click on the **New Report...** button.
2. Select the **Opportunities** report type; it is under the **Opportunities** category.
3. Click on the **Create** button to continue.
4. Change **Show** to **All opportunities**.
5. Change **Date Field** to **Close Date** and **Range** to **Previous CY**.
6. Click on the **Remove All Columns** link, then click on **OK** to confirm, and drag following fields into the report: **Opportunity Name**, **Account Name**, and **Amount**.

7. Click on the **Add** button to add the **Won equals True** filter criteria.

8. Hover your mouse over **Amount**, click on the arrow and select **Summarize the Field...**. Select the sum checkbox to sum **Amount of Opportunity**.

9. Change the report format to **Joined**.

10. Once the report format is changed to **Joined**, the **Add Report Type** button will become available and the opportunity block will be added to the report.

11. Click on the **Opportunities** block label (block 1) and change it to **Won Opportunities Last Year**:

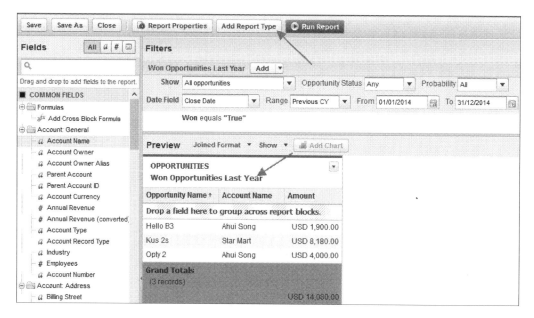

12. Click on the **Add Report Type** button to continue.

13. Select the **Cases** report type under the customer support reports category, and click on **OK** to continue.

14. Remove all the fields from the case block, except **Subject** and **Account Name**.

15. Click on the block labeled **Cases block 2** and change it to **All Cases Last Year**.

16. In the case filter, leave **Date Field** as **Opened Date** and change **Range** to **Previous CY**. If you do not see the case filter, grab the horizontal bar and drag it to a lower position:

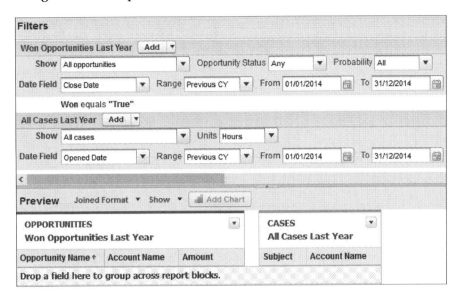

17. From **COMMON FIELDS** to the left, drag **Account Name** into the drop zones. **Account Name** will be automatically removed from both the blocks:

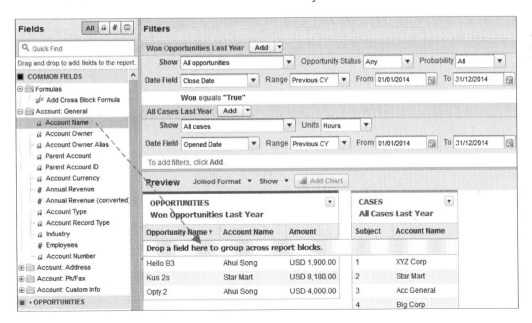

18. By default, **Show Details** will be enabled; let's disable it for now. Click on the **Show** menu and uncheck **Details**.

19. Click on the **Run Report** button. You should see a joined report like what is shown in the following screenshot:

	OPPORTUNITIES Won Opportunities Last Year		CASES All Cases Last Year
	Record Count	Amount	Record Count
Account Name: Acc General			1
Account Name: Ahui Song	2	USD 5,900.00	1
Account Name: Big Corp	1	USD 85,200.00	1
Account Name: Firing Air			1
Account Name: Global Data	1	USD 15,000.00	2
Account Name: Kisaran Corp			1
Account Name: Star Mart	1	USD 8,180.00	1
Account Name: XYZ Corp			1
Grand Totals	5	USD 114,280.00	9

20. Click on the **Show Details** button to show the opportunity and case details.

21. Click on the **Save As** button:

   ○ Report Name = Last Year Won Opportunities with Cases

   ○ Report Description = All Accounts for Last Year closed Won opportunities and Cases

   ○ Report Folder = My Personal Custom Reports

This report will show the count of all won opportunities with the sum of amounts and cases for the previous year, grouped by account name.

Here are a few notes about joined reports:

- To use a joined report as the data source in a dashboard, make sure a chart is added to the report and select **Use charts as defined in source report** in the dashboard settings

- Each report type can be added only once to the report, but you can use the same report type for multiple blocks

- To add new blocks using the same report type, drag the field into the report area, further to the right of the last block

Adding a chart to a report

Adding a chart in a report is good practice for users to get a quick glance of the report's data, and for better visualization. You can add a chart to any report format, except a tabular report. However, a tabular report with a row limit and dashboard settings allows itself to be used as the data source report for the dashboard.

The chart type for a report

Out of the box, there are six types of charts available in Salesforce reports. Differentiate charts in a report from dashboard components, which we will discuss in *Chapter 6, Creating Your First Dashboard*.

Let's cover each of them in the following sections.

Horizontal bar chart

Select the **Horizontal Bar Chart** type when you have many values on the *y* axis. You can have up to four bars for each *x* axis, depending on the summarized field in the report, for example, the pipeline report based on the sum of closed won and the sum of forecast for each sales representative. If we have 20 sales representatives, the charts will be still looking good and not too crowded.

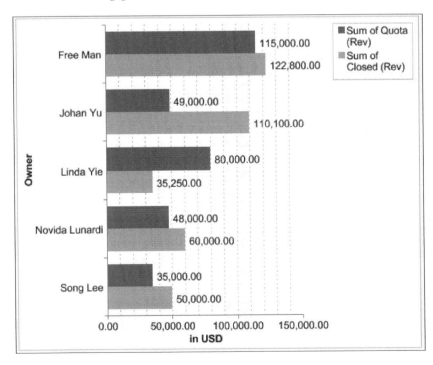

Vertical bar chart

A vertical bar chart is similar to a horizontal bar chart. This chart is good when the number of groupings is small, for example, a calendar month in a year. Just as in horizontal bar chart, you can add multiple bars here, based on the summarized field in the reports.

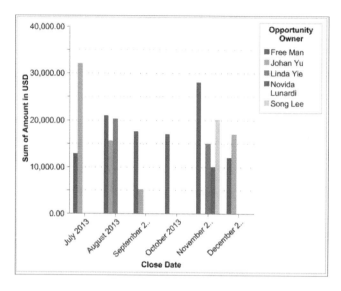

Line chart

Line charts are good for showing changes in the values of an item over a series of points in time. You can have up to two lines in one line chart:

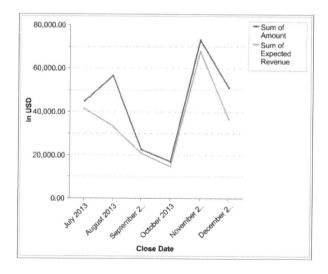

Pie chart

A pie chart is good to show the percentage of each group against the total in one glance. Reader will be able to quickly understand which group has the biggest portion and the smallest portion:

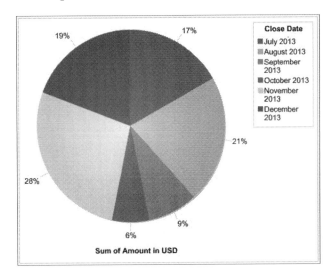

Donut chart

A donut chart is almost similar to a pie chart, where reader is able to notice the biggest portion and the smallest portion in a glance, furthermore the donut chart also shows the total value, for example, the pipeline report by stage with the total value:

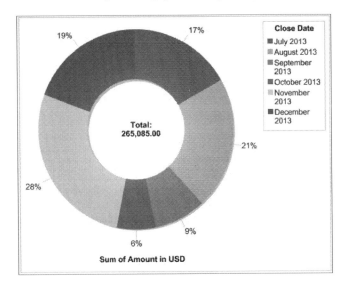

Funnel chart

A funnel chart is good to show values of groups in an order based on a grouping field, for example, the total value of each opportunity stage with the order of sales process:

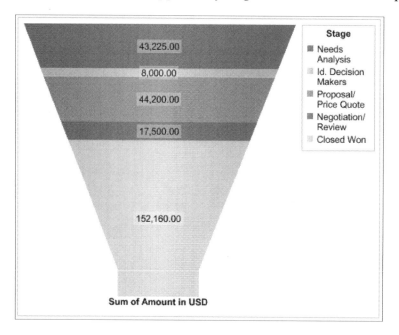

Hands-on – adding a chart to a report

In this exercise, we will create an opportunity report grouped by opportunity stage in a summary format. Let's walk through the steps we need to take:

1. Navigate to the **Reports** tab and click on the **New Report...** button.
2. Select the **Opportunities** report type. It is under the opportunities category.
3. Click on the **Create** button to continue.
4. Change **Show** to **All Opportunities**.
5. Change the **Date Field** section's **Range** value to **All Time**.
6. Click on the **Remove All Columns** link to clear all the default fields added to the report.
7. Change the report format to **Summary**.

8. Drag the following fields into the report: **Opportunity Name**, **Amount**, and **Expected Revenue**. To find the field name quickly, type the field name in the field textbox and double-click on the field to get it added to the report.

9. Drag the **Stage** field into the grouping drop zone.

10. Add all the preceding fields with **Sum**.

11. Click on the **Add Chart** button.

12. Select **Vertical Bar Chart**, as we do not have too many stages.

13. In the **Chart Data** tab, select **Y-Axis** as **Sum of Amount** and **X-Axis** as **Stage**. Select **Plot additional values**, as shown in the following screenshot. Then select **Display** as **Column** and **Value** as **Sum of Expected Revenue**.

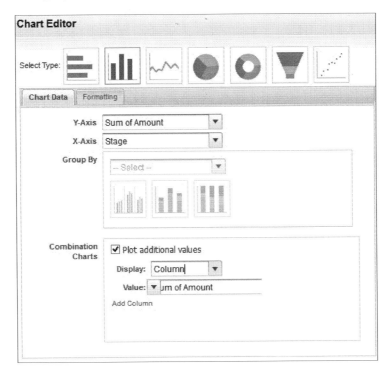

14. In the **Formatting** tab, enter **Chart Title** as **Opportunity Amount by Stage**. Select **Enable Hover** and leave the rest of the items at their default values.

15. Click on **OK** and then navigate to **Run Report | Hide Details**.

16. Click on the **Save As** button:

    ○ Report Name = All Opportunities by Stage with Chart

    ○ Report Folder = My Personal Custom Reports

You should see a chart similar to what is shown in the following screenshot added to your report:

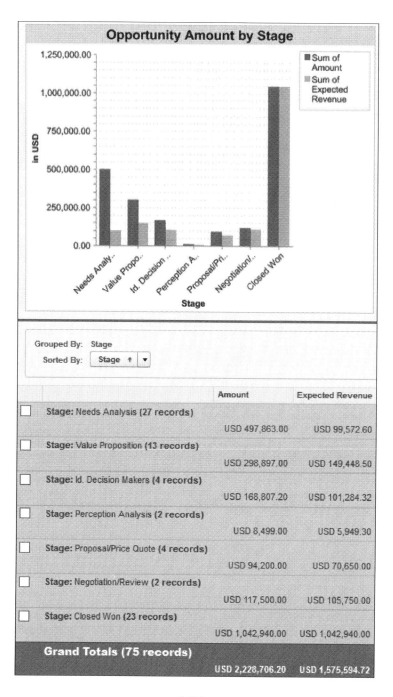

Working with report filters

The report is one of the most powerful features of the Salesforce platform. Depending on your permission, as a business user, you can build your own reports within minutes, and manage them without help from any Salesforce administrator or developer.

We have discussed many things related to reports, such as permissions to create reports; permissions related to the report folder; the report type, which determines objects and fields available for reports; and the report format, which provides the report layout.

Another important item related to reports is the report filter. Report filters allow us to define which data conditions we want to use to include records in a report based on some criteria. The filter criteria in reports are almost similar to the filter criteria we found in list views, workflow rules, and other areas in Salesforce, but filter criteria in reports are more powerful.

For each filter criteria, you need to set the field, operator, and value. You can have multiple filters for a report. The default relationship for each filter using AND, but you can customize it using filter logic.

When you are in **Report Builder**, clicking on the **Add** button for filters will automatically add a new filter. Notice the small arrow button next to **Add**. If you click on it, a few options become available for the report filter:

- **Field Filter**, which is the same action as clicking on the **Add** button
- **Filter Logic**
- **Cross Filter**
- **Row Limit** (only for the tabular format)

The following screenshot displays all of these options:

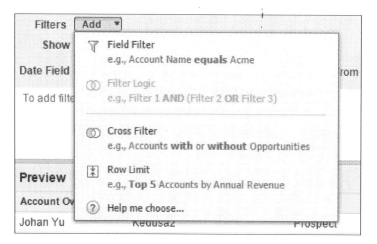

Field Filter

Simply click on the **Add** button in the report builder to add a field as the filter, or you also can drag fields from the **Fields** area to the **Filters** area to add report filter.

Once the field is added to the **Filters** area, select the operator and then enter a value.

 If you would like to add multiple values as filter values, simply use commas to separate the values.

For each filter, you can enter special values, based on the field type for that particular filter. Some points about filters that you need to know are as follows:

- The filter value is case-insensitive.

- For a filter on the date field, you can enter special date values such as `TODAY`, `NEXT WEEK`, `LASTWEEK`, `LAST <x> DAYS`, `LAST <x> YEARS`, and so on. For complete date formats and date literals, refer to `http://www.salesforce.com/us/developer/docs/officetoolkit/Content/sforce_api_calls_soql_select_dateformats.htm`.

- To filter using values with commas, put quotation marks around the text, for example, `"Johan, LLC"`; otherwise, it will filter as `"Johan"` or `"LLC"`.

- If you want to implement multicurrency, you can use currency codes in the filter criteria, such as `SGD 8000` and `JPY 10000`.

- For the picklist field, you can use the magnifying glass to select one or more choices to be included in the filter, or you can manually type them. But when you edit the filter again, the existing selected values will not be selected when you use magnifying glass. If the existing values are no longer valid, delete them manually from the textbox.
- For multiselect picklist fields, use a semicolon between values to specify an exact match.

 If you do not have access to a field defined as a filter, it will be removed from the filter criteria, and results based on the remaining filters will be displayed.

Filter Logic

If you have more than one filter in a report, adding filter logic will let you specify conditions for your filters using logical operators between the filters. When you add filters to a report, all filters will be related with AND logic by default, for example:

- **Type** equals **Customer**
- **Country** equals **United States**
- **Employee** greater than **1000**

This is how they will look when you configure them in Salesforce:

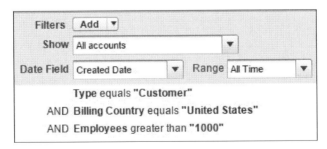

You might have noticed that **AND** will be added to the new filter line by default. With filter logic, you can specify the use of the AND, OR, and NOT operators.

With the preceding filter criteria, the reports will generate all accounts with **Type** equal to **Customer**, **Country** equal to **United States**, and **Employees** more than **1000** people. But, what if we would like to get all accounts with **Type** equal to **Customer** and **Country** equal to **United States**, or **Employees** more than **1000** people, where the last filter does not depend on **Type** and **Country**?

Without filter logic, we need to create two separate reports and combine them manually: one report with the **"Type** equals **Customer AND Country** equals **United States"** filter, and another report with the **"Employee** greater than **1000"** filter.

When we use filter logic, we can combine them into one report by adding **OR** to the filter logic. We can easily modify the filter to meet the requirement: **(Type** equals **"Customer" AND Country** equals **"United States") OR Employee** greater than **"1000"**, as shown in the following screenshot. Use the opening and closing parentheses to let the system calculate which filters should come first. This also helps us understand the filter logic easily.

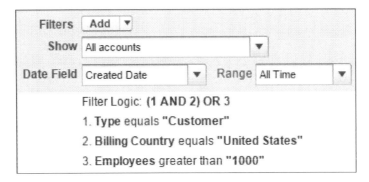

Within seconds, our report will produce the data as required; see how easy and powerful filter logic is!

Hands-on – using Filter Logic

Our next use case is about showing all accounts with **Type** as **Customer** and **Country** as **United States** or **United Kingdom**, We also want to include accounts with employees more than 1,000 people, regardless of the **Account Type** and **Country** values:

1. Navigate to the **Reports** tab and click on the **New Report...** button.

2. Select the **Accounts** report type. It is under the **Accounts & Contacts** category.

3. Click on the **Create** button to continue.

4. Change **Show** to **All Accounts**.

5. Change the **Date Field** section's **Range** value to **All Time**.

6. Click on the **Add** button and select **Type** as **Customer**, since **Type** is the picklist field. You can click on the magnifying glass icon to select the **Customer** value.

7. Click on the **OK** button to confirm the filter.

8. Type `Country` in the **Fields** textbox to the left, drag **Billing Country** into the filter area, and enter `United States, United Kingdom`.

9. Click on the **OK** button to confirm the filter:

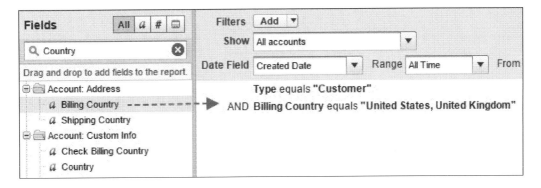

10. Type `Employees` in the **Fields** textbox to the left, and drag it into the filter area.

11. Change the operator to greater than and enter the value `1000`.

12. Click on the **OK** button to confirm the filter.

13. In **Filters**, click on the arrow next to the **Add** button and select **Filter Logic** as shown here:

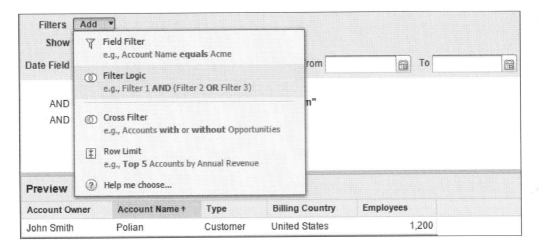

14. The default filter logic value is **1 AND 2 AND 3**. Change it to
    `(1 AND 2) OR 3`.

15. Click on the **OK** button and then on the **Run Report** button to generate
    the report.

16. Click on the **Save As** button:

    ○ Report Name = Account with Filter Logic

    ○ Report Description = All Accounts with No of Employee more than
      1000, or Customer in US or OK

    ○ Report Folder = My Personal Custom Reports

You can enhance the preceding filter logic as long as you use the right pair of the
parentheses with the correct values and operators.

Another thing you learned in this exercise is adding commas in filter values; simply
add a comma in the filter value if you have more than one value, such as **Billing
Country** equals **United States, United Kingdom**.

Here is a screenshot of the final result of the report according to the requirements.
You can click on the **Edit** button to modify the filters added, delete existing filters,
or add more filters.

Filtered By:**(1 AND 2) OR 3**   Edit
  1. **Type** equals **Customer**
  2. **Billing Country** equals **United States,United Kingdom**
  3. **Employees** greater than **"1,000"**

Account Owner	Account Name ↑	Type	Billing Country	Employees
Johan Yu	Aboot Insurance	Customer	United States	800
John Smith	Flow Inc.	Prospect	Singapore	1,250
Johan Yu	Jakarta Raya	Customer	Indonesia	1,540
Johan Yu	PC Show	Customer	United States	325
John Smith	Polian	Customer	United States	1,200

Cross Filter

With **Cross Filter**, you can create reports for an object with dependencies on other objects and their fields. You can use the **WITH** keyword, such as **All Account WITH Opportunity**. Furthermore, you can use the **WITHOUT** keyword for an exception report, such as **Account WITHOUT Closed Won Opportunity this year**. This report is important for the sales manager and management team to evaluate dormant customers.

 This filter will not be available in the joined format report or any report where the report type does not allow optional related objects.

Hands-on – using Cross Filter

Without any further explanation, let's walk through how to create cross filters in a report. Our use case is about showing all accounts with **Type** is **Customer** and have opportunities:

1. Navigate to the **Reports** tab and click on the **New Report…** button.
2. Select the **Accounts** report type; it is under the **Accounts & Contacts** category.
3. Click on the **Create** button to continue.
4. Change **Show** to **All Accounts**.
5. Change the **Date Field** section's **Range** value to **All Time**.
6. Click on the **Add** button and select **Type** as **Customer**, since **Type** is the picklist field. You can click on the magnifying glass icon to select the **Customer** value.
7. Click on the **OK** button to confirm the filter.
8. In **Filters**, click on the arrow next to the **Add** button and then select **Cross Filter**.

9. Select **Accounts**, **with**, and **Opportunities**, as shown in this screenshot:

10. Click on the **OK** button to confirm the filter and on the **Run Report** button to generate the report.

11. As this is a new report, the **Save** button is not available. Click on the **Save As** button to save the report:

    ○ Report Name = Last Year Won Opportunities with Cases

    ○ Report Description = All Accounts for Last Year closed Won opportunities and Cases

    ○ Report Folder = My Personal Custom Reports

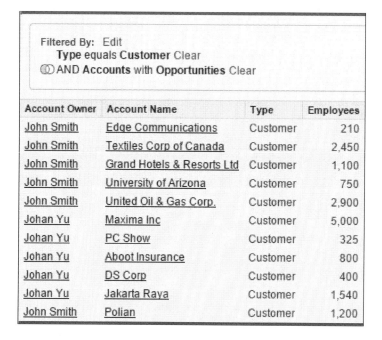

The report will generate all customers with opportunities, but the management would like to limit it only for accounts with the following:

- **Won Opportunity**
- **Opportunity Close Date** within the last 1 year

Let's use the same report and customize it:

1. Open the report and click on the **Customize** button.
2. Click on the **Edit** link in the **Accounts with Opportunities** filter.
3. Click on the **Add Opportunities Filter** link.
4. Select **Won equals True**, since this is the picklist field. You can use the magnifying glass icon to select the value.
5. Click on the **Add Opportunities Filter** link again.
6. Enter **Close Date** greater or equal to **LAST 365 DAYS**. Using the **Relative Date** value is good because it makes the report dynamic and not hardcoded with a value.
7. Click on the **OK** button to confirm the filter and then on the **Run Report** button to generate the report.

The following report will generate all **Customers with Opportunity** outcomes where **Closed Won Date** would be within the last one year from the **Today** date:

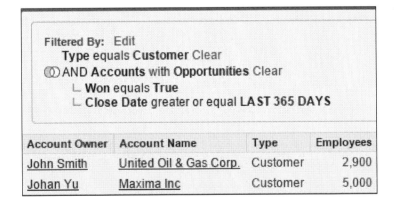

Hands-on – more scenarios using Cross Filter

Let's see a few more scenarios using **Cross Filter** with related objects and their fields used as the filters.

Here is our use case: the management would like to get a list of customers without won opportunities, including customers without opportunities:

- **Customer with Won Opportunities** is **True** will produce a list like this:

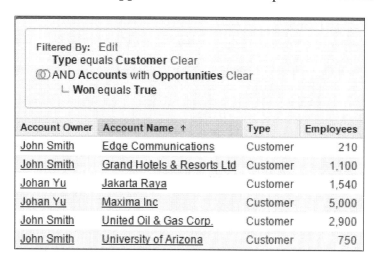

- **Customer with Won Opportunities** is **False** will produce the following list:

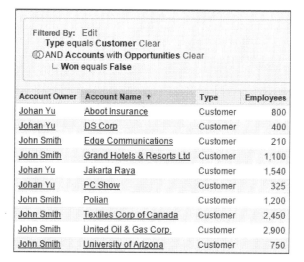

Notice that a few accounts — **Edge Communications, Grand Hotels & Resorts Ltd, Jakarta Raya, United Oil & Gas Corp.,** and **University of Arizona** — are shown in both the preceding reports. This is because those accounts have opportunities with the **Closed Won** stage and also opportunities that are either still **Open** or **Closed Lost**. Remember that one account may have multiple opportunities.

For this use case, **Cross Filter** will not be the right approach. The solution is to use a roll-up summary field in an account and add it to the filter logic.

Let's walk through the steps we need to take:

1. Create a roll-up summary field in the account; let's call it `No of Won Opportunity`.

2. **Summarized Object** is given the **Opportunities** value. The summary type is **Count** and **Filter Criteria** is **Won equals True**:

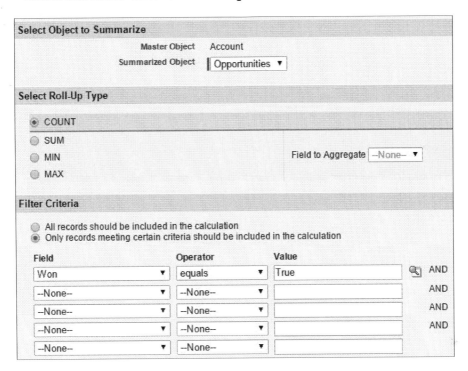

3. Create the report shown in the following screenshot to use **No of Won Opportunity** as a report filter:

Filtered By: Edit
   Type equals **Customer** Clear
   AND **No of Won Opportunity** equals **0** Clear

Account Owner	Account Name	Type	Employees
Johan Yu	DS Corp	Customer	400
Johan Yu	Aboot Insurance	Customer	800
John Smith	Bandung Lake	Customer	75
John Smith	Textiles Corp of Canada	Customer	2,450
John Smith	United Oil & Gas, UK	Customer	2,100
John Smith	United Oil & Gas, Singapore	Customer	4,400
John Smith	Polian	Customer	1,200
Johan Yu	PC Show	Customer	325
John Smith	Apa View	Customer	500
Johan Yu	美好的一天	Customer	1,400
John Smith	Kisaran Inc	Customer	780

This report shows us that not all scenarios are fit for using **Cross Filter** with additional filters.

Row Limit

The **Row Limit** filter is available only for tabular reports; if you are using summary, matrix, or joined format reports, it will not be available.

Once you've added a row limit to a tabular report, you can configure the dashboard settings. From the dashboard settings, choose a name and value to use in the dashboard tables and charts. Tables show both the name and the value, while charts are grouped by name.

A tabular report with dashboard settings configured can be used as the data source in the dashboard component.

Hands-on – adding row limit and dashboard settings

Now we have to create a report that shows the five accounts with the most number of employees, and configure the report as the data source for the dashboard:

1. Navigate to the **Reports** tab and click on the **New Report...** button.
2. Select the **Accounts** report type; it is under the **Accounts & Contacts** category.
3. Click on the **Create** button to continue.
4. Change **Show** to **All Accounts**.
5. Change the **Date Field** section's **Range** value to **All Time**.
6. Remove unwanted default fields from the report, and leave only **Account Owner** and **Account Name**.
7. Add the **Employees** field by dragging and dropping it into the report area.
8. In **Filters**, click on the arrow next to the **Add** button and select **Row Limit**.
9. Change **Row Limit** to 5, and change the **Sorted By** value from **Account Owner** as **Ascending** to **Employees** as **Descending**:

10. Click on the **OK** button. You will notice that the **Dashboard Settings** button appears in the top row next to the **Run Report** button.
11. Click on the **Dashboard Settings** button.
12. Select **Account Name** for **Name** and **Employees** for **Value**, and click on the **OK** button. Once the dashboard settings are configured, this report can be used as the data source in the dashboard component. We'll discuss dashboards in *Chapter 6, Creating Your First Dashboard*, in more detail.

13. Click on the **Run Report** button. You should see something similar to what is shown in the following screenshot:

Limited Display: Limited to **5 rows**, sorted **Descending** by **Employees** Clear		
Account Owner	**Account Name**	**Employees**
Johan Yu	Jakarta Raya	1,540
Yujohan Pengirim	Flow Inc.	1,250
Yujohan Pengirim	Polian	1,200
Yujohan Pengirim	Adil Corp	500
Yujohan Pengirim	Ace Iron and Steel Inc.	220
Grand Totals (5 records)		

14. Click on the **Save As** button to save the report:

   ° Report Name = Top 5 Accounts by Employee

   ° Report Description = Top 5 Accounts with most number of employees

   ° Report Folder = Unfiled Public Reports, it would be visible for other users based on their data accessibility

Managing custom report types

In *Chapter 3, Creating Your First Report*, we discussed report types and how to create a custom report type. Now we will go deeper into the report type and how to manage it.

Creating a report type view

If you are familiar with View in Salesforce in the tab, **Report Types** offers the same view functionality for the administrator to easily manage the report type:

1. Navigate to **Setup | Create | Report Types**.

2. Click on the **Create New View** link.

3. Enter **View Name** as **Others**.

4. In the filter criteria, select **Category** as **Other Reports**.

5. You can add or remove the selected fields.

6. Click on **Save**.

Customizing a report type

In this topic, we assume that a custom report type called **Survey Report Type** has been created. This report type consists of a survey object as the primary object, and the recipient as the related object. The survey records may or may not be related to recipient records.

When you create a report type, this is what happens by default:

- All fields from the primary objects and the related objects will be added to the report type, except the lookup field from related to parent, but you can add the fields from the related object

- Only parent object names and related object names will be added by default to the reports column

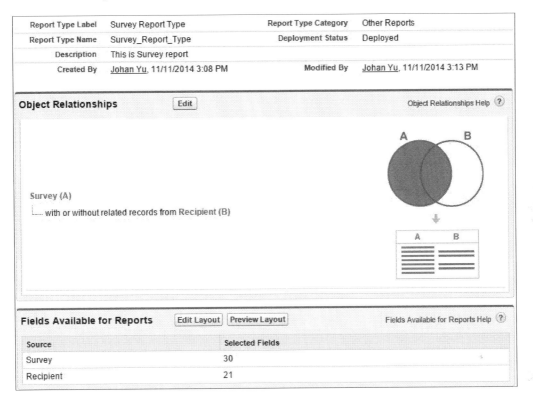

When users use this report type to create a report, they will see the **Survey** and **Recipient** fields in the **Fields** panel, which is available in **Report Builder**, as shown in the following screenshot:

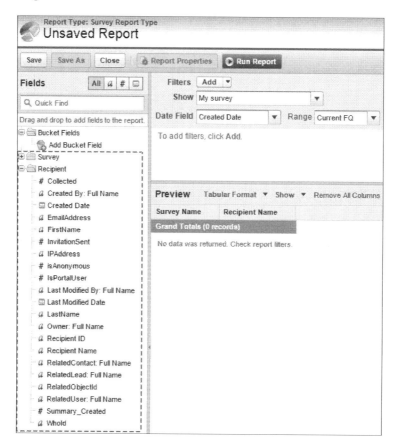

Count the number of fields available for **Survey** and **Recipient**. It should be the same as the number of fields we saw earlier in the report type definition page: 30 for **Survey** and 21 for **Recipient**.

Removing fields from the report type

While removing fields from a report type, we would like to remove some fields from the **Survey** report type. The requirement is to make those fields unavailable in **Report Builder**. Let's walk through the steps for this scenario:

1. Navigate to **Setup | Create | Report Types**.
2. Click on the report type named **Survey Report Type**.

3. Click on the **Edit Layout** button in the fields available for the reports-related list.

4. Drag and drop the field you want to remove into the right panel. Fields removed will be shown in the right panel with darker text and a different background color:

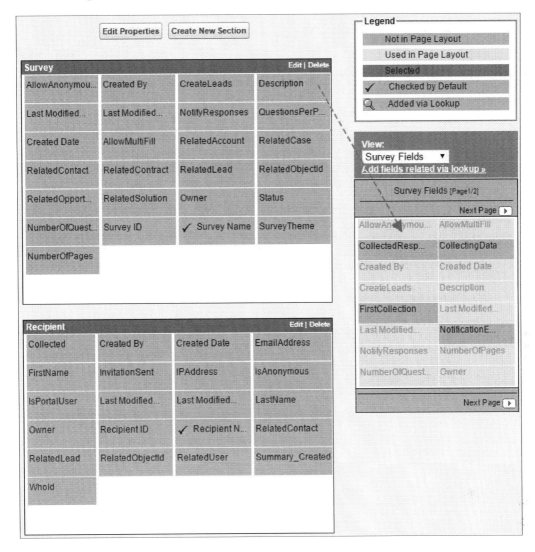

5. Click on the **Save** button to return to the report type summary page.

A field removed from a report type will be not available when a user uses that report type to create a report.

 For existing reports, if the field used in the report is removed from its report type, that field will be deleted from the report filters and report data. This can make existing reports invalid, so only remove fields from report types that are in use after you have removed the fields from the reports themselves.

Managing default field visibility

When you create a new report, Salesforce will put a few default fields in the tabular report format. If the report is built on the custom report type, we can add or remove the default fields by following these steps:

1. Navigate to **Setup | Create | Report Types**.
2. Click on the report type named **Survey Report Type**.
3. Click on the **Edit Layout** button in the fields available for the reports-related list.
4. Double-click on a field in the field layout properties, for example, **Status**, and check **Checked by Default**, as shown in this screenshot:

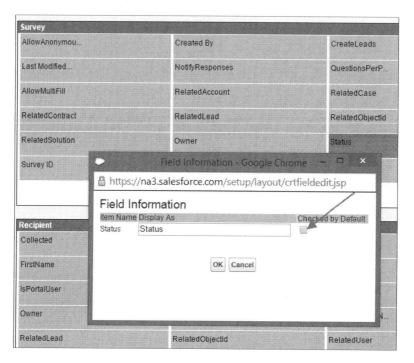

5. Click on the **Save** button.

6. Now, create a new report using **Survey Report Type**. You should see that the **Status** field is added by default to the report, as shown in the following screenshot:

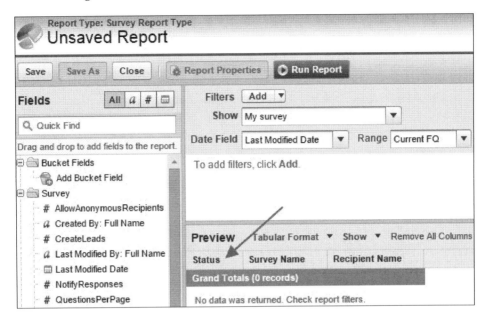

Adding a lookup field to a report type

While adding a lookup field to a report type, we would like to add the survey owner's e-mail address as an available field when the user creates a survey report. By default, only the owner name is available for reports, while the owner's e-mail does not exist directly in survey objects.

Let's walk through this scenario with the following steps:

1. Navigate to **Setup** | **Create** | **Report Types**.

2. Click on the report type named **Survey Report Type**.

3. Click on the **Edit Layout** button in the fields available for the reports-related list.

4. In the right panel, click on the **Add Fields Related to Survey Via Lookup** link.

5. Select **Owner** and then **E-mail**, as shown in this screenshot:

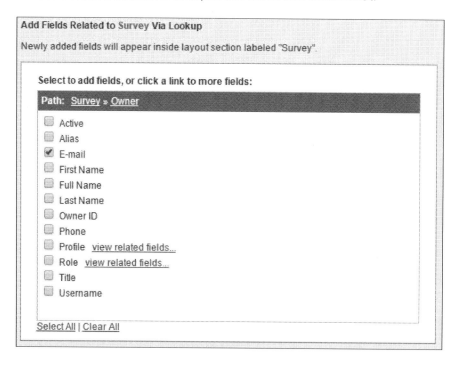

6. Click on **OK** and then on the **Save** button.

7. Create a new report again, using the same report type. You should see the **Owner: E-mail** field available for the report:

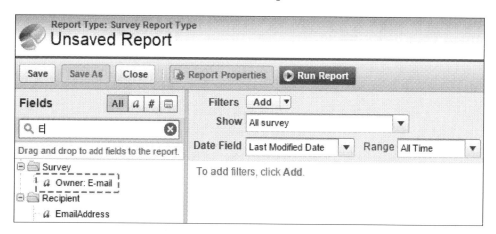

Hiding a report type

Not all report types created, including the standard report type provided by Salesforce, are useful to the user. Too many report types often confuse the user about using the right report type. In this scenario, we would like to hide some report types. Hiding a report type does not mean deleting it permanently. This exercise is applicable only for users with the **Manage Custom Reports** permission.

Here are the steps required to hide the report type so that it won't be available for the user:

1. Navigate to the **Reports** tab.
2. Click on the **New Report...** button.
3. Click on the **Select Report Types to Hide** checkbox.
4. Click on + on the report type category to see all report types for that category.
5. Click on the green icon near the report type name; it will change to a yellow cross, which means it will be no longer available for use:

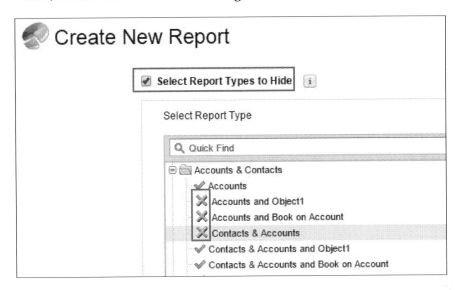

The report is automatically saved.

When the user clicks on a new report, report types with the yellow cross icon, as shown the preceding screenshot, will not be visible anymore.

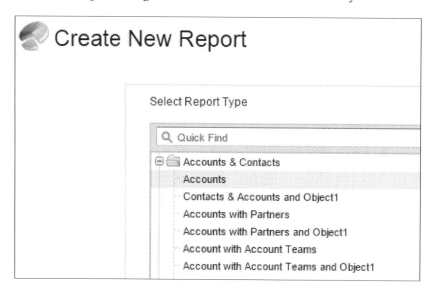

 Existing reports built on the report type marked as hidden will not be affected.

Analyzing the usage of report types

Over time, we may have created many report types for different purposes. But how often are those report types used?

We can run a report to analyze usage of the report type, but this is only for reports saved in the Public report folders. Reports in My Personal Custom Reports are not visible to anyone, including the administrator, so we cannot analyze them.

When you create a report for report usage, included report type used for the report, you may see some of the reports from the My Personal Custom Reports folder. Note that those reports are only the ones that exist in your personal folder, not in every user personal folder.

Let's walk through the steps to create a report of available reports with the report type:

1. Navigate to the **Reports** tab.

2. Click on the **New Report...** button.

3. Select the report type as **Report with Report Type**, and click on the **Create** button to continue.

4. Change **Show** to **All reports**.

5. Change **Created Date** to **All Time**.

6. Add the following fields to the report:

   ○ **Report Name**

   ○ **Report Type**

   ○ **Folder: Name**

   ○ **Created By: Full Name**

   ○ **Created Date**

   ○ **Last Run**

7. The orders are sorted by report type in ascending order, as shown in the following screenshot:

Report Name ↑	Report Type	Folder: Name	Created By: Full Name	Created Date	Last Run
Account summary	Opportunities	Unfiled Public Reports	Johan Yu	12/29/2013	8/31/2014 4:51 PM
Account type won matrix	Opportunities	Unfiled Public Reports	Johan Yu	12/29/2013	8/31/2014 4:51 PM
Account won	Opportunities	Unfiled Public Reports	Johan Yu	11/29/2013	6/4/2014 7:24 AM
Account won matrix	Opportunities	Unfiled Public Reports	Johan Yu	12/29/2013	2/23/2014 4:42 PM
All contacts	Contacts & Accounts	My Folder 1	Johan Yu	8/23/2012	10/19/2014 6:06 AM
All Field Analyses	Custom Object with Custom Object	Field Trip Reports	Johan Yu	6/18/2013	-
All Recent Activity by Campaign	Custom Object with Custom Object	MailChimp for Salesforce	Johan Yu	11/6/2014	-

With this report, you can analyze the use of each report type by comparing the count of reports for a particular report type. Customize it and turn it into a summary or matrix report to understand which report types are used most often.

You will also see who created the report, when it was created, where it is stored, and when the last run was. This information should be enough when you have a report cleanup activity in the organization.

Be careful when you delete the report types that have been deployed. Deleting a report type will also result in the following:

- Permanently delete the custom report type.
- Delete all the reports built on the custom report type. If the report type is used in a joined report, the joined report could end up as invalid as well.
- Dashboard components will result in an error when supporting reports are deleted.

When you change the report type deployment status from **Deployed** to **In Development**, it will make the reports built on that report type inaccessible. Insufficient privileges: you do not have the level of access necessary to perform the operation you requested. Contact the owner of the record or your administrator if access is necessary. The same for dashboard built on the affected reports will become error.

Subscribing to a report

Subscribing to a report is a new feature in Salesforce introduced in the Spring 2015 release. When you subscribe to a report, you will get a notification on weekdays, daily, or weekly, when the reports meet the criteria defined. You just need to subscribe to the report that you most care about.

Subscribing to a report is not the same as the report's **Schedule Future Run** option, where scheduling a report for a future run will keep e-mailing you the report content at a specified frequency defined, without specifying any conditions.

But when you subscribe to a report, you will receive notifications when the report output meets the criteria you have defined. Subscribing to a report will not send you the e-mail content, but just an alert that the report you subscribed to meets the conditions specified.

To subscribe to a report, you do not need additional permission as our administrator is able to control to enable or disable this feature for the entire organization. By default, this feature will be turned on for customers using the Salesforce Spring 2015 release. If you are an administrator for the organization, you can check out this feature by navigating to **Setup | Customize | Reports & Dashboards | Report Notification | Enable report notification subscriptions for all users**.

Besides receiving notifications via e-mail, you also can opt for Salesforce1 notifications and posts to Chatter feeds, and execute a custom action.

Report subscription

To subscribe to a report, you need to define a set of conditions to trigger the notifications. Here is what you need to understand before you subscribe to a report:

- **When**: Everytime conditions are met or only the first time conditions are met.

- **Conditions**: An aggregate can be a record count or a summarize field. Then define the operator and value you want the aggregate to be compared to. The summarize field means a field that you use in that report to summarize its data as average, smallest, largest, or sum. You can add multiple conditions, but at this moment, you only have the AND condition.

- **Schedule frequency**: Schedule weekday, daily, weekly, and the time the report will be run.

- **Actions**:
  - **E-mail notifications**: You will get e-mail alerts when conditions are met.
  - **Posts to Chatter feeds**: Alerts will be posted to your Chatter feed.
  - **Salesforce1 notifications**: Alerts in your Salesforce1 app.
  - **Execute a custom action**: This will trigger a call to the apex class. You will need a developer to write apex code for this.

- **Active**: This is a checkbox used to activate or disable subscription. You may just need to disable it when you need to unsubscribe temporarily; otherwise, deleting will remove all the settings defined.

The following screenshot shows the conditions set in order to subscribe to a report:

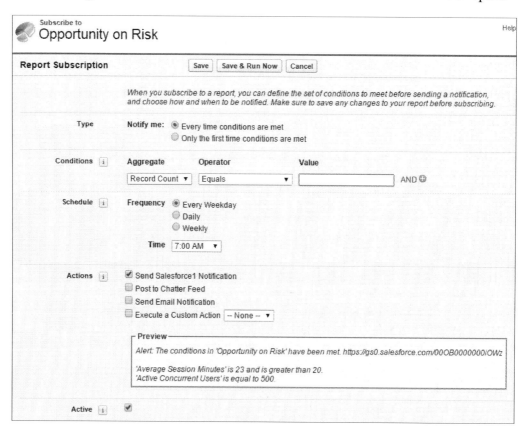

Monitoring a report subscription

How can you know whether you have subscribed to a report? When you open the report and see the **Subscribe** button, it means you are not subscribed to that report:

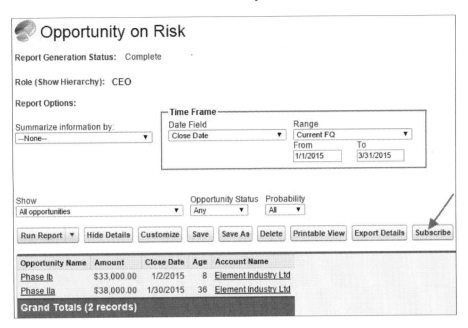

Once you configure the report to subscribe, the button label will turn to **Edit Subscription**. But, do not get it wrong that not all reports with **Edit Subscription**, you will get alerts when the report meets the criteria, because the setting may just not be active, remember step above when you subscribe a report.

To know all the reports you subscribe to at a glance, as long as you have **View Setup** and **Configuration** permissions, navigate to **Setup | Jobs | Scheduled Jobs**, and look for **Type** as **Reporting Notification**, as shown in this screenshot:

Hands-on – subscribing to a report

Here is our next use case: you would like to get a notification in your Salesforce1 app—an e-mail notification—and also posts on your Chatter feed once the **Closed Won** opportunity for the month has reached $50,000. Salesforce should check the report daily, but instead of getting this notification daily, you want to get it only once a week or month; otherwise, it will be disturbing.

Creating reports

Make sure you set the report with the correct filter, set **Close Date** as **This Month**, and summarize the **Amount** field, as shown in the following screenshot:

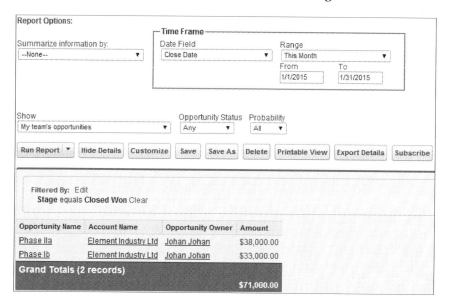

Subscribing

Click on the **Subscribe** button and fill in the following details:

- **Type** as **Only the first time conditions are met**
- **Conditions**:
  - **Aggregate** as **Sum of Amount**
  - **Operator** as **Greater Than or Equal**
  - **Value** as **50000**
- **Schedule**:
  - **Frequency** as **Every Weekday**
  - **Time** as **7AM**
- In **Actions**, select:
  - **Send Salesforce1 Notification**
  - **Post to Chatter Feed**
  - **Send Email Notification**
- In **Active**, select the checkbox

Testing and saving

The good thing of this feature is the ability to test without waiting until the scheduled date or time. Click on the **Save & Run Now** button. Here is the result:

Salesforce1 notifications

Open your Salesforce1 mobile app, look for the notification icon, and notice a new alert from the report you subscribed to, as shown in this screenshot:

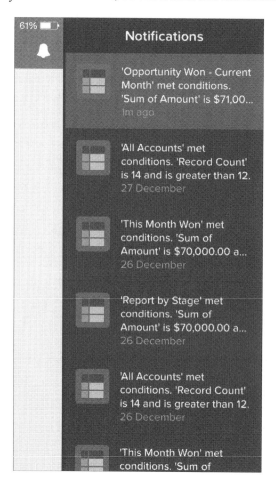

If you click on the notification, it will take you to the report that is shown in the following screenshot:

Chatter feed

Since you selected the **Post to Chatter Feed** action, the same alert will go to your Chatter feed as well. Clicking on the link in the Chatter feed will open the same report in your Salesforce1 mobile app or from the web browser, as shown in this screenshot:

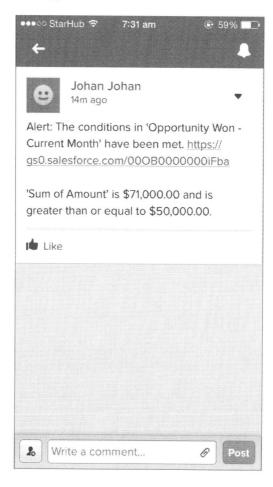

E-mail notification

The last action we've selected for this exercise is to send an e-mail notification. The following screenshot shows how the e-mail notification would look:

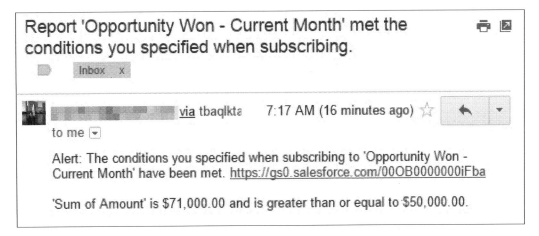

Limitations

The following limitations are observed while subscribing to a report:

- You can set up to five conditions per report, and no OR logic conditions are possible
- You can subscribe for up to five reports, so use it wisely

Summary

In this chapter, you became familiar with components when working with reports on the Salesforce platform. We saw different report formats and the uniqueness of each format. We continued discussions on adding various types of charts to the report with point-and-click effort and no code; all of this can be done within minutes.

We saw how to add filters to reports to customize our reports further, including using **Filter Logic**, **Cross Filter**, and **Row Limit** for tabular reports. We walked through managing and customizing custom report types, including how to hide unused report types and report type adoption analysis. In the last part of this chapter, we saw how easy it is to subscribe to a report and define criteria.

Although we hinted at dashboards many times in this chapter, we have not discussed them in this chapter; dashboards will be discussed from *Chapter 6, Creating Your First Dashboard* onwards. This chapter was entirely based on reports.

In the next chapter, we will discuss advanced report configuration, including custom summary formulas, field buckets, schedule reports, and how to embed a chart from a report in a record page layout.

5
Learning Advanced Report Configuration

In *Chapter 3*, *Creating Your First Report*, we discussed various permissions related to reports and report folders, and in the same chapter, we saw how to create reports from scratch. In *Chapter 4*, *Working with Reports*, we continued our discussion on components that are required when creating and working with reports, including selecting the right report format, adding charts to reports, working with report filters, and managing custom report types.

This chapter will be the last chapter in this book that discusses reports in Salesforce. We will discuss more functionalities when working with reports in Salesforce. The following topics will be covered in this chapter:

- Categorizing data in reports
- Working with the custom summary formula
- Scheduling reports
- Adding embedded report charts

Categorizing data in reports

You learned about using the summary report format to group reports into multiple levels with available fields. Reports will be shown in groups, with the number of groups depending on the values returned for the fields used in grouping.

What if we need to put multiple values of a field into one category? Creating a formula field with a CASE() function may be one of the solutions, but think about how often that formula field will be used, maybe just for a report. Is the category standard for the entire organization, or only for a report?

If the answer is only for one or a smaller number of reports, and it is not standard for the whole organization, then creating a new formula field is not a good solution. Furthermore, there is a maximum number of formula fields that you can create in an object, depending on your Salesforce edition. The bucket field comes into the picture for the preceding scenarios.

The bucket field

So what is a bucket field? It is a functionality offered by Salesforce only in reporting. It lets you quickly categorize values for a field in a report without creating a custom formula field at the object level. When you create a bucket field, you define multiple categories in groups depending on the record values; this bucket field will not affect other reports or the object itself.

For example, suppose you have the following values in the **Account** type:

- **Prospect**
- **Customer-Direct**
- **Customer-Channel**
- **Channel Partner/Reseller**
- **Installation Partner**
- **Technology Partner**
- **Other**

You need to categorize all account types containing customers as **Customer**, all account types containing partners as **Partner**, all account types containing prospects as **Prospect**, and the rest as **Other**. By using a bucket field, you will get a new field in the report without having to create the field in the account object just for this purpose. The bucket field will contain the following values:

- **Prospect**
- **Customer**
- **Partner**
- **Other**

These values are only applicable for that particular report.

Bucket fields are available in all report formats: tabular, summary, and matrix. When you change the report format to any of the other formats, the bucket fields will stay the same. But the joined report does not support bucket fields. If you have any report with a bucket field and you change the report to a joined report, the bucket field will be removed.

You can add up to five bucket fields in a report; each bucket field can contain up to 20 buckets.

You can use the following field types as the source fields for the bucket field:

- Number, currency, or percent
- Picklist
- Text
- Lookup

This includes the formula field and roll-up summary field with the return type as stated in the preceding points.

The following fields cannot be used as source fields for a bucket field:

- **Date** and **Date/Time**; you still can use a concept similar to bucket fields by using the **Group By** feature, which we discussed in summary and matrix reports
- **Checkbox**; you can create a custom formula text field that returns `Yes/No` or `True/False`, and use that custom field in the bucket field
- **Email**
- **Phone**
- **Picklist** (multiselect)
- **Text Area**, **Long Text Area**, and **Rich Text Area**
- **URL**

Adding a bucket field to reports

Create an account report and categorize all account types containing customers as **Customer**, all account types containing partners as **Partner**, all account types containing prospects as **Prospect**, and the rest as **Other**. You need to perform the following steps:

1. Navigate to the **Reports** tab and click on the **New Report...** button.
2. Select the **Accounts** report type; it is under **Accounts & Contacts** category.
3. Click on the **Create** button to continue.
4. Change **Show** to **All Accounts**.

5. Change the **Date Field** section's **Range** value to **All Time**.

6. Click on **Remove All Columns** to clear the report without any columns. This link is useful when you want to create a new report without a default field.

7. Add **Account Name** and **Account Owner** to the report by double-clicking on the field from the left panel.

8. Double-click (or drag these columns into the report area) on **Add Bucket Field** at the top-left panel under **Bucket Fields**.

9. Select **Source Column** as **Type**.

10. In **Bucket Field Name**, enter Type (Core).

11. Click on the **New Bucket** button and type Customer; repeat all the preceding steps for **Partner** and **Prospect**.

12. Select all types that contain **Customer**, click on the **Move To** button, and then select **Customer**. You will notice a bucket label added to the picklist selected. Repeat this step for **Partner** and **Prospect**.

13. Tick **Show Unbucketed values as "Other."** to categorize the rest as **Other**.

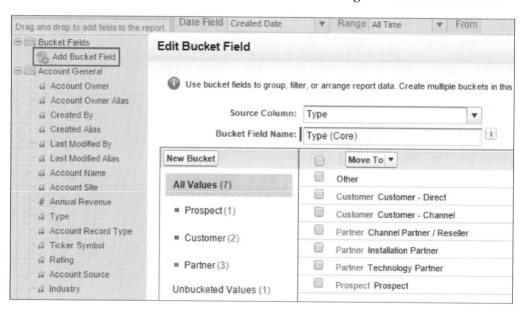

14. Click on the **OK** button to continue. You will notice a new column called **Type (Core)** added to the report, with a bucket icon before the label. Click on the **Run Report** button to continue, as shown in this screenshot:

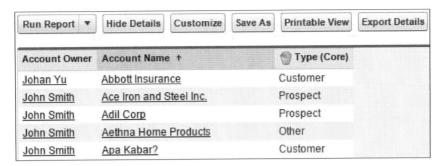

15. Click on the **Save As** button. Enter the report name as `Account with Bucket Fields`. Save the report in the `My Personal Custom Reports` report folder.

You can treat the bucket field as a normal field in the following ways:

- Use as a grouping in summary and matrix reports
- Use as a report filter
- Use for report sorting
- It is available when we export reports via **Printable View** and **Export Details**
- It is included in field search results when you type in the left panel to filter the fields

Creating a bucket field based on the source field type

In the preceding example, we used a picklist field as the source field, but different field types will require different ways to define a bucket field.

We will discuss how we can create bucket fields using different types of fields as the field source.

Picklist fields

Using a bucket field with picklist as the field source, you will be able to categorize the picklist values into fewer values. Here are a few points to note when creating a bucket field with picklist field as the source field:

- Select the picklist value and move it into the buckets

- Not all picklist fields can be used as the source for buckets

- If you do not select **Show unbucketed values as "Other."**, all values not captured in the bucket will appear as original picklist value. The following screenshot of the bucket field shows use of picklist field type as source data:

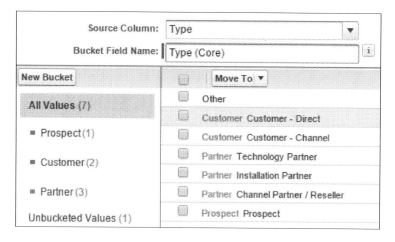

The currency, number, and percent fields

Using a bucket field with currency, number, and percent types of fields as the field source, you will be able to sort data that can be described in terms of numbers. The following are a few points to note when creating the bucket field with these type of fields as the source field:

- You must have a minimum of two buckets for both small- and big-range values

- You can add many bucket ranges in between two buckets for up to a total of 20 buckets

- If you do not tick **Treat empty Acc No values in the report as zeros**, blank values of the source column will appear as blank value. The following screenshot of the bucket field shows the use of these type of fields as source data:

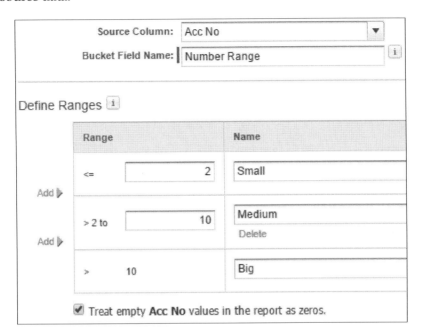

The text and lookup fields

Using a bucket field with the text and lookup type of fields as the field source, you will be able to categorize based on values that consist of words or phrases. Here are a few points to note for a bucket field with this source field type:

- Search for the text value of the source column; all values containing the search keyword will be shown. Note that it is case-insensitive. Or, click on the **Enter Values** tab to manually enter values and move into the bucket.

- Select the search result and move into the bucket.

- If you do not tick **Show Unbucketed values as "Other."**, all values not captured in the bucket will appear as original value. The following screenshot of the bucket field shows the use of these type of fields as source data:

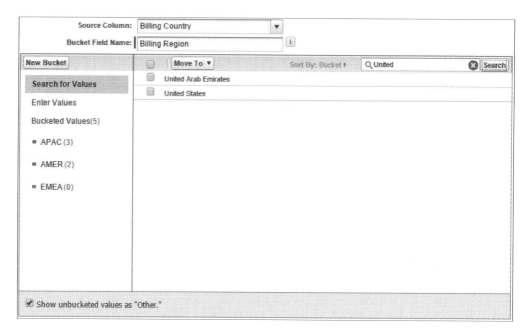

Editing a bucket field

You can edit bucket fields by hovering your mouse over the bucket field and then clicking on the pencil icon. You can delete a bucket field by clicking on the trash bin icon.

Clicking on the pencil icon will open the bucket field window. To remove selected values from the bucket value, you need to perform the following steps:

1. Click on the bucket value; it will show all the values selected for that bucket.
2. Click on the selected values.

3. Click on the **Move To** button and then select **Unbucketed Values** or a different bucket, as shown in this screenshot:

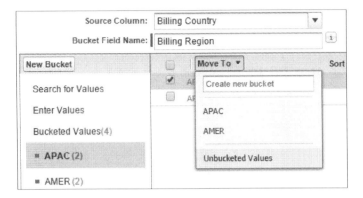

Working with custom summary formula fields

Custom summary formula is a powerful reporting technique used to create summaries of your numerical fields. This only available for summary, matrix, and joined reports. A custom summary formula offers you the ability to calculate additional totals based on the numeric fields available in the report, including the record count. Like bucket fields, custom summary formula fields created in a report will only be available in that report; they will not affect any other reports and database, and you cannot use or refer them to other reports.

 Do not confuse custom summary formulas in reports with custom formula fields in objects; they are totally different things and are not related at all, although both have formulas.

When you need to get values from a lookup field in the report, a custom formula field is the answer. You cannot use a custom summary formula for this purpose. One of the options is to create a custom formula field in the object and hide it from the page layout.

The options for the format return from custom summary formulas are as follows:

- Currency
- Number
- Percent

When you create a custom summary formula field, you also need to define how many decimal points for that summary formula field.

As with the return format, only the following field types can be used in a formula for custom summary formula fields. Note that formula fields and roll-up summary fields of these data types can be used as well:

- Currency
- Number
- Percent
- Record count

In a summary report, custom summary formula fields can display the following details:

- All the summary levels; this would be similar to field summarizing
- Grand summary only, which is the grand total
- Grouping, in level one, two, or three

Similar to the summarized field in reports, you also can do the same for summary formula fields: sum, max, min, and average. When you add `Summarize this Field...` in a summary or matrix report, Salesforce will calculate on the field you are summarizing. A custom summary formula field not only provides the same summarizing as **Summarize this Field...**, but it also lets you create more complex summary information, for example, **Account.Number_of_Branch__c:SUM / RowCount**.

Some points to take note of from the summary formula field are as follows:

- It will be always shown in the last column of the report. If you have multiple formulas, it will be ordered by when the formula was created.
- You cannot summarize the summary formula field.

 If you change the report format, the formula summary field in the report will be deleted, so be careful.

Adding a simple summary formula

For the following use case, we would like to generate a report to show all open opportunities with the total of **Amount** and grouped by **Opportunity Owner**. Let's name the report `Open Opportunities`.

You need to perform the following steps:

1. Navigate to the **Reports** tab and click on the **New Report...** button.

2. Select the **Opportunities** report type; it is under the **Opportunity** category.

3. Click on the **Create** button to continue.

4. Change **Show** to **All opportunities**.

5. Change the **Date Field** section's **Range** value to **All Time**.

6. Change **Format** to **Summary**, and remove all columns.

7. Add **Opportunity Name**, **Account Name**, and **Amount** to the report.

8. Drag **Opportunity Owner** into the grouping area.

9. Enter the **Filters** value as `Closed equals False`.

10. Double-click on **Add Formula** in the left panel.

11. Enter the column name as `Total Open Opportunities`.

12. Select **Format** as **Currency** and **Decimal Places** as **2**.

13. Select **All summary levels**.

14. In the formula, navigate to **Summary Fields | Amount | Sum**.

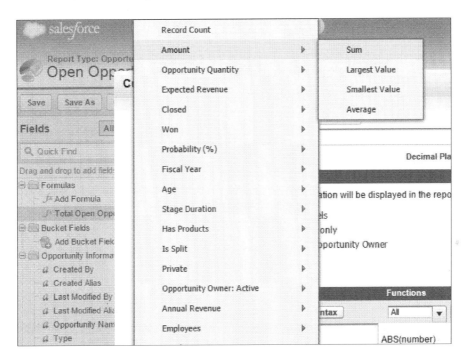

The formula will be automatically filled with **AMOUNT:SUM**.

15. Click on the **OK** button to continue. Notice that **Total Open Opportunities** is added to **Formulas** in the report, as shown in the following screenshot. Click on the **Run Report** button to continue.

Opportunity Name	Account Name ↑	Amount	Total Open Opportunities
Opportunity Owner: Johan Yu **(8 records)**			
		$207,300.00	$207,300.00
Baru Phase-I	Baru Inc.	$18,000.00	
Baru Phase-II	Baru Inc.	$25,000.00	
Hello Part-1	Hello Corp	$17,000.00	
Hello Part-2	Hello Corp	$21,000.00	
Hello Part-3	Hello Corp	$9,800.00	
Jayabaya 2 Mph	Jayabaya	$19,000.00	
Maya-1	Maya Inc.	$80,000.00	
Drill in Sub-Ocean	United Oil & Gas Corp.	$17,500.00	
Opportunity Owner: John Smith **(3 records)**			
		$26,100.00	$26,100.00
New Datapipe	Bink Co	$7,000.00	
Jakarta-Stage 2	Jakarta-1	$9,000.00	
Qaa-II	Qaa Inc	$10,100.00	
Grand Totals (11 records)			
		$233,400.00	**$233,400.00**

16. Notice that the total open opportunities summary formula field is the same as the summary of the **Amount** field.

17. Click on the **Save As** button, and provide values as follows:

    ° **Report Name** as Open Opportunities
    ° **Report Folder** as My Personal Custom Reports

The preceding report has not shown any powerful usage of the summary formula; we can achieve the same by summarizing the **Amount** field. Nevertheless, this gives us a basic understanding of how the summary formula field works. In the summary formula field, we can define the field shown in any of the following:

- All summary levels
- Only the grand summary
- Only at any grouping level and not in the grand summary

While, in **Summarize this Field...**, it always shows the total in every grouping and also in the grand total.

The **summary** formula field is always added to the last column of the report and cannot be moved to the left column before the normal field.

To edit or delete the summary formula field, perform these steps:

- Open the report
- Click on the **Customize** button to open Report Builder
- Hover your mouse over the summary formula field
- Click on the pencil icon to edit or the trash bin icon to delete

Using the summary formula field

In the preceding exercise, we saw a simple formula called **AMOUNT:SUM**. It just summarizes **Amount** in a group and/or grand total.

Let's continue to look at this custom summary formula field in greater detail.

In the next use case, we would like to add the total expected profit to the preceding report and show only the summary. In the opportunity, we only have a custom currency field, called **Cost**. Let's make an agreement where **Profit** is equal to the difference between amount and cost.

1. Navigate to the **Reports** tab and click on the **Open Opportunities** report.
2. Click on the **Customize** button to open Report Builder.
3. Double-click on the **Add Formula** link and make the following changes:
   - **Column Name: Total Cost**
   - **Format: Currency**
   - **Decimal Places: 2**
   - **Display in: All summary levels**
   - **Formula: Opportunity.Cost__c:SUM**
4. Click on the **OK** button, and **Total Cost** will be added to the last report column.

5. Add another formula with the following details:

   ○ **Column Name: Total Expected Profit**

   ○ **Format: Currency**

   ○ **Decimal Places: 2**

   ○ **Display in: All summary levels**

   ○ **Formula: AMOUNT:SUM - Opportunity.Cost__c:SUM**

   The same happens with the previous exercise to get the preceding formula. Navigate to **Summary Fields | Amount | Sum | Operators | Subtract | Summary Fields | Cost | Sum**.

6. Click on the **OK** button. **Total Profit** will be added to the last report column.

7. Click on the **Run Report** button to continue, and then click on the **Hide Details** button.

	Amount	Total Open Opportunities	Total Cost	Total Expected Profit
Opportunity Owner: Johan Yu (8 records)				
	$207,300.00	$207,300.00	$75,200.00	$132,100.00
Opportunity Owner: John Smith (3 records)				
	$26,100.00	$26,100.00	$15,200.00	$10,900.00
Grand Totals (11 records)				
	$233,400.00	**$233,400.00**	**$90,400.00**	**$143,000.00**

8. Click on the **Save** button to save the report. All the summary formula fields created will be available for this report only, and they do not affect fields at the **Opportunity** level.

In this exercise, we see how to use the summary formula fields to get **Profit**, even though we do not have that field in the **Opportunity** object. For this sample, you do not need to create the **Total Open Opportunities** summary field and **Total Cost** summary field to get the **Total Expected Profit** summary field. They are all independent; just use it to show the correct calculation.

Using operators in the summary formula field

In the previous exercise, we used operators in the formula, where we inserted the subtract operator between two summary formulas. We can use the same procedure with other formulas.

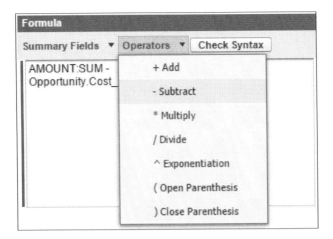

Using functions in the summary formula field

You might have noticed that to the right of the formula in the **Custom Summary Formula** editor, there are many functions available for you to use in the formula. They are categorized as logical, math, and summary. We will not discuss each function available, but let's see a few samples.

IF function

The IF function is categorized as a logical function. The syntax for this is as follows:

```
IF(logical_test, value_if_true, value_if_false)
```

This function checks whether a condition is true. It returns one value if TRUE and another value if FALSE.

Here is an example of this function:

```
IF( AMOUNT:SUM - Opportunity.Cost__c:SUM > 100000, (AMOUNT:SUM
- Opportunity.Cost__c:SUM)  * 0.05, (AMOUNT:SUM - Opportunity.
Cost__c:SUM)  * 0.04)
```

You do not have to type all summary fields manually, such as AMOUNT:SUM and Opportunity.Cost__c:SUM; where you also may not know the right syntax. Just position your cursor in the formula text area and navigate to **Summary Fields** | field name | **Sum**. Once you click on **Sum**, it will automatically populate the formula at the position of your cursor.

You also can insert the formula by selecting the function name, clicking on the **< Insert** button, and then deleting the default values for each parameter. In the preceding sample, we used a custom summary field to calculate the commission for each user based on the expected profit. If the profit is less than $100,000.00, the user will get a 5 percent commission from the profit. Otherwise, they will get only 4 percent. Let's see how the report will look. Since we only need the commission for each user, we select to display the summary formula field in the grouping level only.

	Amount	Total Expected Profit	Total Expected Commision
Opportunity Owner: Johan Yu (8 records)			
	$207,300.00	$132,100.00	$6,605.00
Opportunity Owner: John Smith (3 records)			
	$26,100.00	$10,900.00	$436.00
Grand Totals (11 records)			
	$233,400.00	$143,000.00	

Let's analyze the preceding report:

- We remove **Total Open Opportunities** and **Total Cost** to show that each summary formula field is independent
- For the owner **Johan Yu**, since the total expected profit is more than $100,000.00, the commission will be 5 percent of the total profit
- For the owner **John Smith**, since the total expected profit is less than or equal to $100,000.00, the commission will be 4 percent of the total profit
- We set **Total Expected Commission** to display only at the grouping level, as commission is not become applicable for the grand total

MAX function

The MAX function is categorized as a math function. Here is its syntax:
MAX(number,number,...).

This function returns the greatest of all the arguments. The following is an example of this function: MAX (Opportunity.Amount_Number__c:SUM, AMOUNT:SUM).

Like the IF function in the preceding section, you can just point and click to get the formula populated. In this sample, the formula will return the maximum number by comparing the sum of **Amount** with the sum of a custom field called **Amount_Number__c**.

Opportunity Name	Close Date	Amount (converted)	Amount Number	Max Amount
Opportunity Owner: Lea Smith - Adil (5 records)				
		SGD 339,457.52	337,150.00	SGD 339,457.52
Greenwich Media-Book Acquisition	31/03/2013	SGD 10,457.52	8,150.00	
GenePoint SLA	14/03/2012	SGD 110,000.00	110,000.00	
GenePoint Standby Generator	28/04/2012	SGD 85,000.00	85,000.00	
Antenna Fix 1 Year	20/07/2012	SGD 89,000.00	89,000.00	
Hotel Adia-Medan Two	31/08/2012	SGD 45,000.00	45,000.00	
Opportunity Owner: Milis Dua Penerima (3 records)				
		SGD 79,673.20	84,750.00	SGD 84,750.00
KA comp-Cisaa Wireless	03/10/2013	SGD 49,673.20	44,100.00	
Jup-Jampalan One	06/08/2013	SGD 5,000.00	4,950.00	
SCD-Foreign Extra	27/05/2012	SGD 25,000.00	35,700.00	
Grand Totals (8 records)				
		SGD 419,130.72	421,900.00	

Let's analyze the preceding report. **Max Amount** is a summary formula field:

- We set the **Max Amount** display only at the grouping level
- Since there are multiple currencies in the report, we use the converted amount in SGD instead of amount in the original currency
- For the owner **Lead Smith – Adil**, the converted amount is greater than **Amount Number**, so **Max Amount** is equal to the converted amount
- For the owner **Milis Dua Penerima**, it is the other way round; **Amount Number** is greater than the converted amount

Relative functions formula

There are two functions in Salesforce that are available only in the summary formula and are considered as the most powerful formulas for a report summary. They are categorized as summary functions: PARENTGROUPVAL() and PREVGROUPVAL().

PARENTGROUPVAL()

The PARENTGROUPVAL() function returns the value of a specified grouping. The grouping level is higher than the formula display level.

The formula syntax is different, depending on the report format:

- In summary and joined reports, it is PARENTGROUPVAL(summary_field, grouping_level)

- In a matrix report, it is PARENTGROUPVAL(summary_field, parent_row_grouping, parent_column_grouping)

The summary_field parameter is similar to other summary formula functions. You can just point and click on the summary fields, select the field name, and then select the summarizing action.

To use the PARENTGROUPVAL() function in the summary report, note the following:

- If the report has only one level of grouping, where the formula has to be displayed, you should select **Grouping 1** only, not **All summary levels** or **Grand summary only**. **Grand summary** will be the only option used to define the parent grouping level.

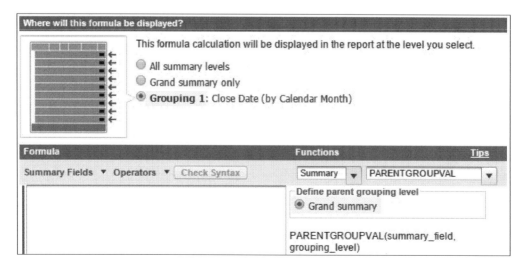

- Suppose the report has more than one level of grouping, where the formula has to be displayed, you should select **Grouping 1** or **Grouping 2**, not **All summary levels** or **Grand summary only**. If you select to display in **Grouping 1**, **Grand summary** will be the only option that can be used to define the parent grouping level. Notice that **Close Date** is disabled, as shown in the following screenshot:

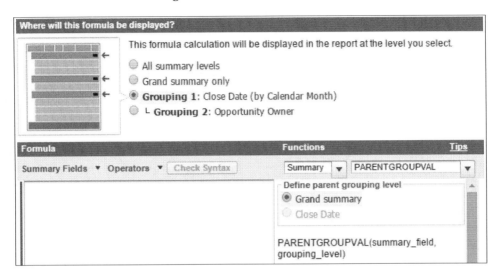

- If you choose to display the formula in **Grouping 2**, **Grand summary** and the level-1 grouping name will be available to define the parent grouping level, as shown in the following screenshot:

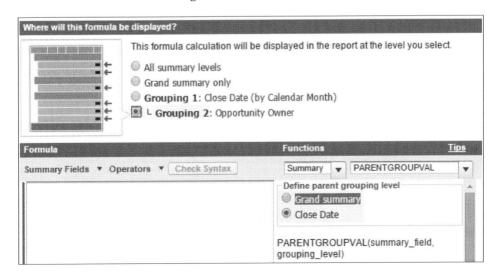

Perform the following steps to populate parameters for PARENTGROUPVAL():

1. Select where the formula has to be displayed. It should be in the grouping level only.

2. Select the **PARENTGROUPVAL** function from the drop-down list of available functions.

3. Define the parent grouping level radio button if your selection to display the formula is not at **Grouping 1**. Otherwise, only **Grand summary** will be available.

4. Click on the **< Insert** button. You will get the formula created, for example, PARENTGROUPVAL(summary_field, CLOSE_DATE).

5. Delete the summary_field parameter and replace it with the correct summary field by clicking on **Summary Fields**.

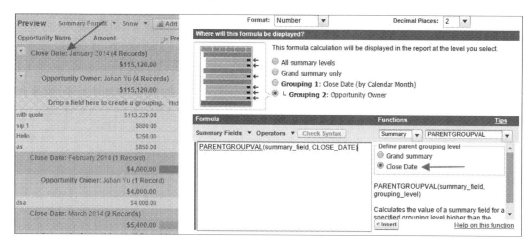

Let's get hands-on with this function. Create a simple opportunity report. Group it by the month of **Close Date** and then by **Opportunity Owner**. A summary formula field called **Amount by Close Date** is used to get the total amount on the monthly **Close Date** (first-level grouping) into **Opportunity Owner** (second-level grouping). You need to perform the following steps:

1. Navigate to the **Reports** tab and click on the **New Report...** button.

2. Select the **Opportunities** report type; it is under the **Opportunity** category.

3. Click on the **Create** button to continue.

4. Change **Show** to **All opportunities**.

5. Change the report to the **Summary** format.

6. Remove all fields from the report. Then add **Opportunity Name** and **Amount**.

7. Group by **Close Date** as the first grouping and **Opportunity Owner** as the second grouping.

8. Replace the **Close Date** grouping with grouping by **Calendar Month**.

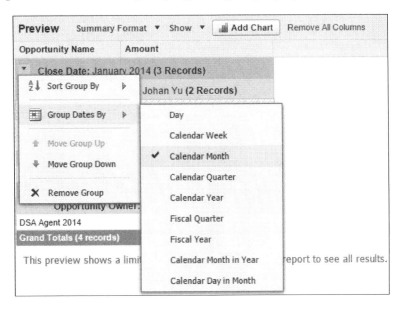

9. Summarize the **Amount** field with **Sum**.

10. Double-click on **Add Formula**. The following details will be added to the dashboard:

    ° **Column Name**: Amount by Owner

    ° **Format**: Currency

    ° **Decimal Places**: 2

    ° **Display**: Grouping 2: Opportunity Owner

    ° Select **PARENTGROUPVAL** under **Summary Function**, and define the parent grouping level as **Close Date**

11. Click on the **< Insert** button. You will get the formula populated as
    PARENTGROUPVAL(summary_field, CLOSE_DATE).

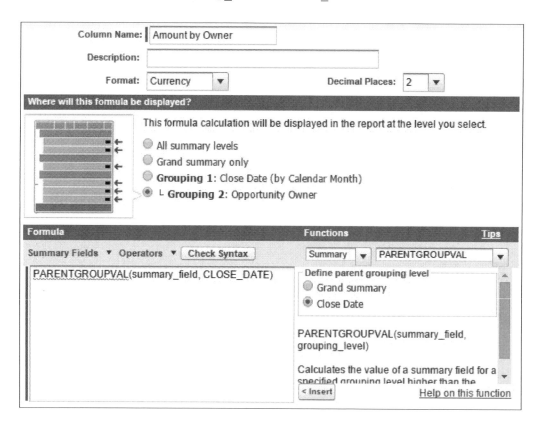

12. With the mouse arrow on the **summary_field** parameter in the formula, delete **summary_field** in the parameter.

13. Navigate to **Summary Fields | Amount | Sum**.

14. Click on the **OK** button to continue.

15. **Amount by Owner** will be added to the last column of the report.

16. Click on the **Run Report** button to get the report and then click on the **Save As** button. The details to be entered here are as follows:

    ○ **Report Name**: Summary PARENTGROUPVAL

    ○ **Report Folder**: My Personal Custom Reports

The resulting report is shown in the following screenshot:

Opportunity Name	Amount	Amount by Owner
Close Date: January 2014 (3 records)		
	$10,050.00	
Opportunity Owner: Johan Yu (2 records)		
	$9,250.00	$10,050.00
Haasa-200K Sydney	$9,000.00	
Hello	$250.00	
Opportunity Owner: John Smith (1 record)		
	$800.00	$10,050.00
Jakarta Water 10K	$800.00	
Close Date: February 2014 (2 records)		
	$6,300.00	
Opportunity Owner: Johan Yu (1 record)		
	$4,000.00	$6,300.00
DSA Agent 2014	$4,000.00	
Opportunity Owner: John Smith (1 record)		
	$2,300.00	$6,300.00
Max-Star X fish	$2,300.00	
Grand Totals (5 records)		
	$16,350.00	

The highlighting in yellow and pink is not from the report; we've done that just to highlight the values related to this report. Let's analyze the report with the following points:

- In January 2014, the total amount was $10,050.00. This value is the same as the value in the **Amount by Owner** summary formula field.

- For February 2014, the total amount was $6,300.00. This value is also the same as the value in the **Amount by Owner** summary formula field.

The summary formula will be available in the **Opportunity Owner** grouping, which is level 2, because PARENTGROUPVAL() is configured to CLOSE_DATE, which is a level-1 grouping.

Next, let's create another similar formula called Amount by Close Date, but with the summary field equal to GRAND_SUMMARY. Here is the formula:

PARENTGROUPVAL(AMOUNT:SUM, GRAND_SUMMARY).

You need to perform the following steps:

1. Navigate to the **Reports** tab and open the report created as **Summary PARENTGROUPVAL**.

2. Click on the **Customize** button.

3. Double-click on **Add Formula**. The following details need to be set up:
   - **Column Name**: Amount by Close Date
   - **Format**: Currency
   - **Decimal Places**: 2
   - **Display**: Grouping 1: Close Date (by **Calendar Month**)

4. Select **PARENTGROUPVAL** under **Summary Function**. **Grand Total** will be the only parent grouping level because the formula will be displayed at **Grouping 1**, that is, **Close Date** (by **Calendar Month**).

5. Click on the **< Insert** button, and you will get the formula populated as PARENTGROUPVAL(summary_field, GRAND_SUMMARY).

6. With the mouse arrow on the **summary_field** parameter in the formula, delete the text.

7. Navigate to **Summary Fields | Amount | Sum**.

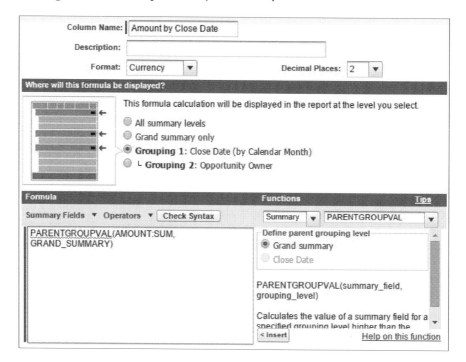

8. Click on the **OK** button to continue.

   Amount by Close Date will be added to the last column of the report.

9. Click on the **Run Report** button to get the report and then click on the
   Save button to overwrite the existing report (Summary PARENTGROUPVAL).
   The resulting report is shown in the following screenshot:

Opportunity Name	Amount	Amount by Owner	Amount by Close Date
Close Date: January 2014 (3 records)			
	$10,050.00		$16,350.00
Opportunity Owner: Johan Yu (2 records)			
	$9,250.00	$10,050.00	
Haasa-200K Sydney	$9,000.00		
Hello	$250.00		
Opportunity Owner: John Smith (1 record)			
	$800.00	$10,050.00	
Jakarta Water 10K	$800.00		
Close Date: February 2014 (2 records)			
	$6,300.00		$16,350.00
Opportunity Owner: Johan Yu (1 record)			
	$4,000.00	$6,300.00	
DSA Agent 2014	$4,000.00		
Opportunity Owner: John Smith (1 record)			
	$2,300.00	$6,300.00	
Max-Star X fish	$2,300.00		
Grand Totals (5 records)			
	$16,350.00		

Let's analyze the report generated with the following points:

- Notice that the values for the summary formula are the same as the
  Grand Totals values.

- The value of the formula is shown in the **Close Date** grouping, which is
  a level -1 grouping because the grouping level is **GRAND_SUMMARY**.
  From the preceding examples, it is clear that the PARENTGROUPVAL() function
  summarizes the grouping values for one level above the current level. Next,
  let's see how the PARENTGROUPVAL() function is used in the matrix report.
  In the matrix report, its syntax is PARENTGROUPVAL(summary_field,
  parent_row_grouping, parent_column_grouping).

The summary field in the matrix report contains two parameters—parent_row_
grouping and parent_column_grouping—whereas the summary report has only
one parameter, which is grouping_level.

Let's create a new opportunity report with the matrix format, filter the report by **Close Date** value of six months, and group it by **Close Date** (and group dates by **Calendar Month**) as column grouping, and use **Stage** as row grouping.

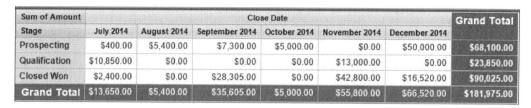

Sum of Amount	Close Date						Grand Total
Stage	July 2014	August 2014	September 2014	October 2014	November 2014	December 2014	
Prospecting	$400.00	$5,400.00	$7,300.00	$5,000.00	$0.00	$50,000.00	$68,100.00
Qualification	$10,850.00	$0.00	$0.00	$0.00	$13,000.00	$0.00	$23,850.00
Closed Won	$2,400.00	$0.00	$28,305.00	$0.00	$42,800.00	$16,520.00	$90,025.00
Grand Total	$13,650.00	$5,400.00	$35,605.00	$5,000.00	$55,800.00	$66,520.00	$181,975.00

In this use case, we would like to know the percentage of each stage compared to the total amount. You need to perform the following steps:

1. Create a formula summary called `Total Amount`. The formula will be displayed under **Column Grand Summary**.

2. Select the formula to be displayed at a specific row or column grouping level by **Stage** and by **Column Grand Summary**.

3. Select the **PARENTGROUPVAL** function in the parent grouping level, and then select **Row Grand Summary**, and **Column Grand Summary**.

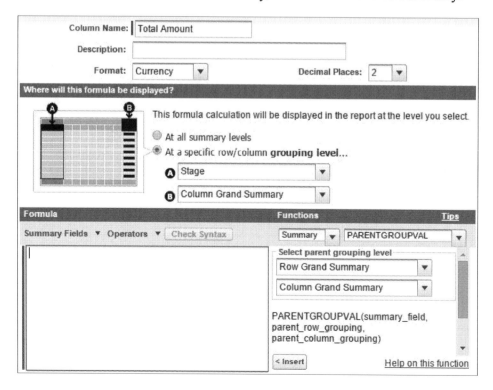

4. Do not worry about how to get the parameter for the summary formula. Once the place where the formula needs to be displayed and the parent grouping level are selected, click on the **< Insert** button to populate the formula with the selected parameters.

5. The `PARENTGROUPVAL(summary_field, ROW_GRAND_SUMMARY, COLUMN_GRAND_SUMMARY)` formula will be populated.

6. Change the `summary_field` parameter to `AMOUNT:SUM`. Delete the `summary_field` parameter. From the right side, navigate to **Summary Fields | Amount | SUM**.

7. Click on **OK** to continue. **Total Amount** will be added to the summarizable field in the matrix report.

8. Click on **Run Report** to see the report shown in the following screenshot:

Stage		July 2014	August 2014	Close Date September 2014	October 2014	November 2014	December 2014	Grand Total
Prospecting	Sum of Amount Total Amount	$400.00	$5,400.00	$7,300.00	$5,000.00	$0.00	$50,000.00	$68,100.00 $181,975.00
Qualification	Sum of Amount Total Amount	$10,850.00	$0.00	$0.00	$0.00	$13,000.00	$0.00	$23,850.00 $181,975.00
Closed Won	Sum of Amount Total Amount	$2,400.00	$0.00	$28,305.00	$0.00	$42,800.00	$16,520.00	$90,025.00 $181,975.00
Grand Total	Sum of Amount	$13,650.00	$5,400.00	$35,605.00	$5,000.00	$55,800.00	$66,520.00	$181,975.00

Total Amount is now added to each total stage, but it does not have much meaning. It just copies the **Grand Total** value to the same cell with each total stage, while we would like to know the percentage of each stage compared to the grand total.

9. Customize the report and edit the summary formula as follows:

    1. Change the name from `Total Amount` to `Total Percentage`.

    2. Change the format to **Percent**.

3. To get the percentage of each stage of **Grand Total**, you need to divide **Stage Total** by **Grand Total**. So, in our case, change the formula to AMOUNT:SUM / PARENTGROUPVAL (AMOUNT:SUM, ROW_GRAND_SUMMARY, COLUMN_GRAND_SUMMARY).

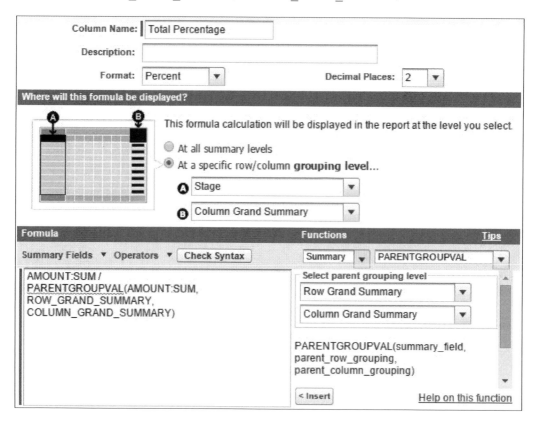

In this exercise, we divide **Stage Total** by **Grand Total** and show the result as a percent value. Here is a screenshot of the report:

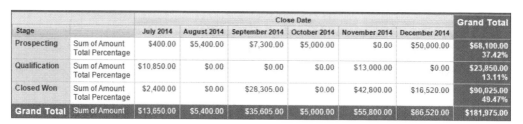

Stage		July 2014	August 2014	September 2014	October 2014	November 2014	December 2014	Grand Total
				Close Date				**Grand Total**
Prospecting	Sum of Amount	$400.00	$5,400.00	$7,300.00	$5,000.00	$0.00	$50,000.00	$68,100.00
	Total Percentage							37.42%
Qualification	Sum of Amount	$10,850.00	$0.00	$0.00	$0.00	$13,000.00	$0.00	$23,850.00
	Total Percentage							13.11%
Closed Won	Sum of Amount	$2,400.00	$0.00	$28,305.00	$0.00	$42,800.00	$16,520.00	$90,025.00
	Total Percentage							49.47%
Grand Total	Sum of Amount	$13,650.00	$5,400.00	$35,605.00	$5,000.00	$55,800.00	$66,520.00	$181,975.00

With a simple change in the **Custom Summary Formula** window, you can also define the formula in the report to get the percentage for each month compared to **Grand Total**. Let's modify the existing report, and instead of getting the percentage of **Stage**, show the percentage of each month.

1. Customize the report and edit the summary formula. Change **A** from the stage to **Row Grand Summary**, and **B** from **Column Grand Summary** to **Close Date (by Calendar Month)**. You can see in the preview window that the formula will be displayed when you select values for **A** and **B**:

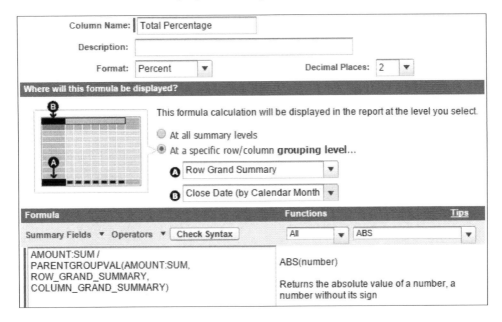

2. Notice that both **A** and **B** have been changed, but the formula stays the same.

3. Click on **OK** to continue. Then click on the **Run Report** button to get the following result:

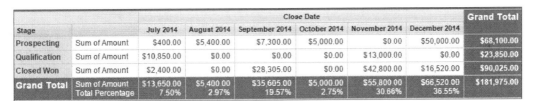

Stage		July 2014	August 2014	September 2014	October 2014	November 2014	December 2014	Grand Total
Prospecting	Sum of Amount	$400.00	$5,400.00	$7,300.00	$5,000.00	$0.00	$50,000.00	$68,100.00
Qualification	Sum of Amount	$10,850.00	$0.00	$0.00	$0.00	$13,000.00	$0.00	$23,850.00
Closed Won	Sum of Amount	$2,400.00	$0.00	$28,305.00	$0.00	$42,800.00	$16,520.00	$90,025.00
Grand Total	Sum of Amount	$13,650.00	$5,400.00	$35,605.00	$5,000.00	$55,800.00	$66,520.00	$181,975.00
	Total Percentage	7.50%	2.97%	19.57%	2.75%	30.66%	36.55%	

You can also modify the summary formula to show the percentage of each cell value compared to **Grand Total** by changing **A** to **Stage** and leaving B at **Close Date (by Calendar Month)**. When you change this, you will notice that the black box will change and show where the formula will be shown in the report.

PREVGROUPVAL()

The PREVGROUPVAL() function returns the value of the previous grouping on the same hierarchy level. This allows Salesforce to prepare reports that show, for example, month-to-month opportunity comparison.

The formula syntax for PREVGROUPVAL() is the same for all report formats: PREVGROUPVAL(summary_field, grouping_level [, increment]).

There is not much difference in the navigation and tips for getting the formula for PREVGROUPVAL(), compared to PARENTGROUPVAL. The only difference in the syntax is an additional optional parameter called incremental. If we skip this parameter, it will use the default value, which is 1. The increment is the number of columns or rows before the current summary. Its minimum and default value is 1 and maximum is 12. Here is a screenshot of a sample report formed when the interval is 1 or is not stated:

	Amount	Prev Value
Close Date: July 2014 (4 records)		
	$13,650.00	
Close Date: August 2014 (1 record)		
	$5,400.00	13,650.00
Close Date: September 2014 (3 records)		
	$35,605.00	5,400.00
Close Date: October 2014 (1 record)		
	$5,000.00	35,605.00
Close Date: November 2014 (6 records)		
	$55,800.00	5,000.00
Close Date: December 2014 (3 records)		
	$66,520.00	55,800.00

The amount of July 2014 is shown in the August 2014 formula, which is one row below July 2014. If we change the interval in the formula to 2 then for the preceding sample, the July 2014 value will be shown two rows below, which is September 2014, as shown in the following screenshot:

	Amount	Prev Value
Close Date: July 2014 (4 records)		
	$13,650.00	
Close Date: August 2014 (1 record)		
	$5,400.00	
Close Date: September 2014 (3 records)		
	$35,605.00	13,650.00
Close Date: October 2014 (1 record)		
	$5,000.00	5,400.00
Close Date: November 2014 (6 records)		
	$55,800.00	35,605.00
Close Date: December 2014 (3 records)		
	$66,520.00	5,000.00

Using the PREVGROUPVAL() function in summary reports is exactly the same as using the PARENTGROUPVAL() function, which we have discussed in depth. So, we will not repeat it again; refer to the PARENTGROUPVAL() function.

Getting the parameters for PREVGROUPVAL() is also similar to PARENTGROUPVAL(). Follow these steps to populate the parameters for PREVGROUPVAL():

1. Select where the formula needs to be displayed. It should be in the grouping level only.

2. Select the **PREVGROUPVAL** function from the drop-down list of available functions.

3. Choose the parent grouping level radio button if your selection to display the formula is not **Grouping 1**. Otherwise, only **Grand summary** will be available.

4. Click on the **< Insert** button. You will get the formula created, for example, PREVGROUPVAL(summary_field, CLOSE_DATE).

5. Delete the **summary_field** parameter and replace it with the correct summary field by clicking on **Summary Fields**.

6. You can manually add a comma and an interval value after the
   `grouping_level` parameter, as shown in the following screenshot:

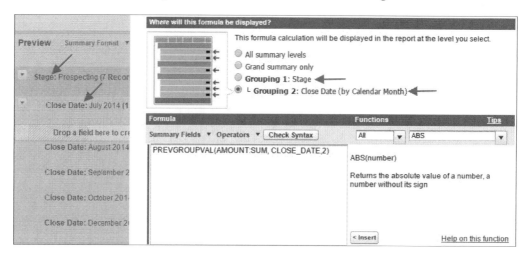

Let's have get hands-on with this function. Create a new opportunity report with the summary format. Group it by **Opportunity Owner** and then by the month of **Close Date**. A summary formula field called **Prev Month Amount** to get the total amount of previous months in the same level of grouping hierarchy can be prepared by performing the following steps:

1. Navigate to the **Reports** tab and click on the **New Report...** button.
2. Select the **Opportunities** report type. It is under the **Opportunity** category.
3. Click on the **Create** button to continue.
4. Change **Show** to **All opportunities**.
5. Change the report to the **Summary** format.
6. Remove all fields from the report. Then add **Opportunity Name** and **Amount**.
7. Group by **Opportunity Owner** as the first grouping and **Close Date** as the second grouping.

8. Change **Close Date** to be grouped by **Calendar Month**.

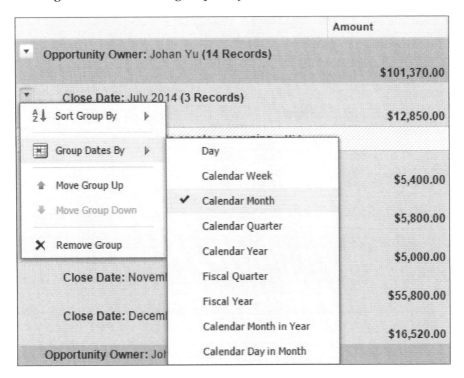

9. Summarize the **Amount** field with **Sum**.

10. Double-click on **Add Formula**. The details will be changed, as follows:

    ° **Column Name**: **Prev Month Amount**

    ° **Format**: **Currency**

    ° **Decimal Places**: **2**

    ° **Display**: **Grouping 2: Close Date (by Calendar Month)**

11. Select **PREVGROUPVAL** under **Summary Function**, and define the parent grouping level as **Close Date**.

12. Click on the **< Insert** button. You will get the formula populated as
    PREVGROUPVAL(summary_field, CLOSE_DATE).

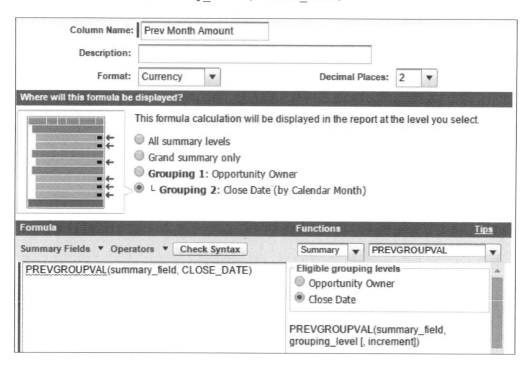

13. With the mouse arrow on the **summary_field** parameter in the formula, delete the text.

14. Navigate to **Summary Fields | Amount | Sum**.

15. Leave the interval parameter because it is optional. Thus, this is the final formula: PREVGROUPVAL(AMOUNT:SUM, CLOSE_DATE).

16. Click on the **OK** button to continue.

    Prev Month Amount will be added to the last column of the report.

17. Click on the **Run Report** button to get the report and then. Then click on the **Save As** button. The following details need to be specified:

    ° **Report name**: Summary PREVGROUPVAL

    ° **Report folder**: My Personal Custom Reports

The resulting report is shown in the following screenshot:

The arrows are not in the report, but are just meant to show how the amount values flow in the report. Let's analyze the report with the following points:

- For the owner named **Johan Yu**, the total amount in **July 2014** is copied to **August 2014** for the summary formula. This is because we leave the optional `Interval` parameter, so 1 will be the default value. It will go for each month until **November 2014**, because for **December 2014**, there is no more summary below it.

- For the owner named **John Smith**, the total amount in **July 2014** is copied to **September 2014** for the summary formula. This is because there is no **August 2014** grouping. Similarly for **September 2014**, the amount goes to **December 2014**. From here, you've learned that `PREVGROUPVAL()` will not know the name of the month or any other common order. It will only copy the value from the previous group's amount by an interval.

Next, let's create another similar summary formula field called **Prev 2 Months Amount**. This summary field will show how an interval works in the PREVGROUPVAL() function. You need to perform the following steps:

1. Navigate to the **Reports** tab and open the report called **Summary PREVGROUPVAL**.

2. Click on the **Customize** button.

3. Double-click on **Add Formula**. The details should be changed as follows:

   ○ **Column Name: Prev 2 Months Amount**

   ○ **Format: Currency**

   ○ **Decimal Places: 2**

   ○ **Display: Grouping 2: Close Date (by Calendar Month)**

4. Select **PREVGROUPVAL** under **Summary Function** and define the parent grouping level as **Close Date**.

5. Click on the **< Insert** button. You will get the formula populated as PREVGROUPVAL(summary_field, CLOSE_DATE).

6. With the mouse arrow on the **summary_field** parameter in the formula, delete the text.

7. Navigate to **Summary Fields | Amount | Sum**.

8. Add the interval value as 2 after CLOSE_DATE.

9. Leave the interval parameter because it is optional, so this is the final formula: PREVGROUPVAL(AMOUNT:SUM, CLOSE_DATE, 2).

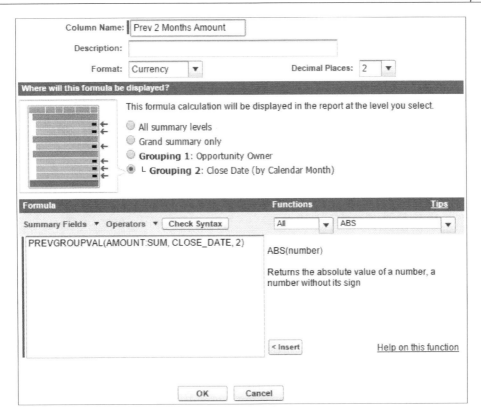

10. Click on the **OK** button to continue.

    Prev 2 Months Amount will be added to the last column of the report.

11. Remove the **Prev Month Amount** summary field, which was created earlier from the report.

Click on the **Run Report** button to get the report and then click on the **Save** button to overwrite the existing report, called **Summary PREVGROUPVAL**. The resulting report is shown in the following screenshot:

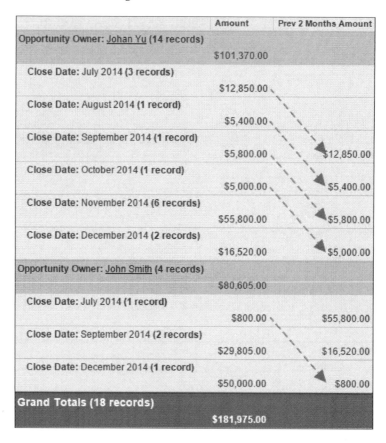

Let's analyze the report generated with the help of the following points:

- Instead of getting the value from the previous grouping, adding an interval of 2 will set the formula to get the value from the two previous groupings.

- Just like the earlier sample, PREVGROUPVAL() does not know the month name or any other common names. It is based on the interval defined where it should get the value. From the two preceding examples, it is clear that the PREVGROUPVAL() function copies the grouping values from the previous groups in the same level of hierarchy, based on the interval defined.

Let's consider the following use case: we would like to get a report to show the percentage of growth of **Total Amount** for each month. You need to perform the following steps:

1. Create a new opportunity report with the matrix format. Group it by **Close Date (by Calendar Month)** with row grouping, and select **Stage** as the column grouping.

2. Create a formula summary called `Month to Month`. Display it at a specific row/column grouping level. Set **A** with **Closed Date (by Calendar Month)** and **B** with **Column Grand Summary**.

3. Set the output format to **Percent** with 2 decimal points.

4. Enter the following formula: `(AMOUNT:SUM - PREVGROUPVAL(AMOUNT:SUM, CLOSE_DATE)) / PREVGROUPVAL(AMOUNT:SUM, CLOSE_DATE)`.

5. Click on the **OK** button to continue and then click on **Run Report** to get the report.

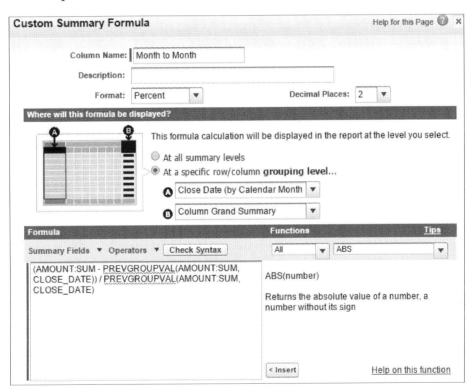

The summary formula will be added to the **Grand Total** column below **Total Amount** for each month. You will notice this when you configure where this formula is to be displayed in the formula summary. The resulting report is as follows:

Close Date		Stage			Grand Total
		Prospecting	Qualification	Closed Won	
July 2014	Sum of Amount Month to Month	$0.00	$10,850.00	$2,400.00	$13,250.00
August 2014	Sum of Amount Month to Month	$0.00	$0.00	$15,000.00	$15,000.00 13.21%
September 2014	Sum of Amount Month to Month	$7,300.00	$0.00	$28,305.00	$35,605.00 137.37%
October 2014	Sum of Amount Month to Month	$5,000.00	$0.00	$0.00	$5,000.00 -85.96%
November 2014	Sum of Amount Month to Month	$0.00	$3,000.00	$6,200.00	$9,200.00 84.00%
December 2014	Sum of Amount Month to Month	$0.00	$0.00	$18,820.00	$18,820.00 104.57%
Grand Total	Sum of Amount	$12,300.00	$13,850.00	$70,725.00	$96,875.00

Notice that no value is shown for **July 2014,** as it was the first value. In **August 2014,** there is an increase of **13.21%** compared to the month before. **October 2014** shows a decrease of **85.96%** compared to **September 2014**.

Adding conditional highlighting

Conditional highlighting is not really related to the summary formula field or relative function. You might notice that under the **Show** drop-down menu in Report Builder, there is a function used to highlight the report values based on some criteria you define.

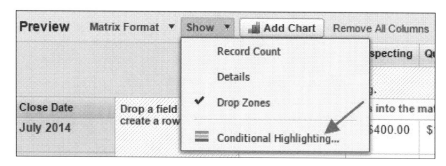

Conditional highlighting allows you to customize your reports by showing visual highlights for analysis and eye-catching effects. It is applicable for reports in summary and matrix formats.

Let's use the last report we built for PREVGROUPVAL(). If the monthly increase is higher than 0 percent, we set the highlight color to green, and if it is below 0 percent, we set the highlight color to red:

1. Navigate to the **Reports** tab and open the report created as **Summary PREVGROUPVAL**.

2. Click on the **Customize** button.

3. Navigate to **Show | Conditional Highlighting…**.

4. Click on the field in the drop-down menu and select **Month to Month**.

5. Enter 0 in both the separators.

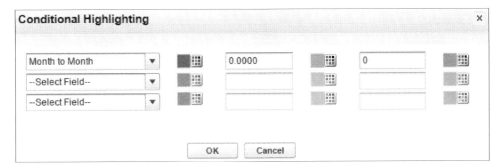

6. Click on the **OK** button to continue. Even before you can click on **Run Report**, you will see the highlighting in **Preview** window.

			Stage		Grand Total
Close Date		Prospecting	Qualification	Closed Won	
July 2014	Sum of Amount Month to Month	$0.00	$10,850.00	$2,400.00	$13,250.00
August 2014	Sum of Amount Month to Month	$0.00	$0.00	$15,000.00	$15,000.00 13.21%
September 2014	Sum of Amount Month to Month	$7,300.00	$0.00	$28,305.00	$35,605.00 137.37%
October 2014	Sum of Amount Month to Month	$5,000.00	$0.00	$0.00	$5,000.00 -85.96%
November 2014	Sum of Amount Month to Month	$0.00	$3,000.00	$6,200.00	$9,200.00 84.00%
December 2014	Sum of Amount Month to Month	$0.00	$0.00	$18,820.00	$18,820.00 104.57%
Grand Total	Sum of Amount	$12,300.00	$13,850.00	$70,725.00	$96,875.00

Scheduling a report

Another great feature offered by Salesforce is the capability to schedule and send reports via e-mail. For users who are not using Salesforce in their daily work but need to see the report periodically, they may sometimes just forget about the report. With the scheduling of reports, an e-mail notification will be sent automatically in HTML format to the recipients defined, but recipients must have an active Salesforce license.

Users with the **Schedule Reports** permission given in **Profile** or **Permission Set** are able to schedule reports for themselves or include other users or just schedule reports for other users. We can define report scheduling frequency as follows:

- **Daily**: This is scheduled every weekday or every day
- **Weekly**: This recurs every week on Monday, Tuesday, Wednesday, Thursday, Friday, Saturday, and Sunday
- **Monthly**: This is scheduled on day X every month, or the Xth day of the month, for example, the first Monday of every month

You can schedule any custom reports except the joined report. To schedule Salesforce standard reports, save the report as a new custom report.

When you schedule a report, you can set a running user, if you have the permissions. This user can be you or someone else. The data shown in the report is based on the accessibility of the user set as the running user.

E-mail recipients

Only users who have access to the report folder are able to receive the e-mail containing reports. If users are unable to access the report, the username will not show up in the list of recipients.

This means reports in the `My Personal Custom Report` folder cannot be sent to other users, but only to you. If you plan to send a report to other users, ensure that the report is located in a public folder and is shared with all the intended recipients.

Reports in **Unfiled Public Reports** are accessible by all users. You can schedule reports in this folder to any users in your Salesforce profile, including Chatter users as long as they are active.

You can set the report recipients to:

- Individual users
- Public groups
- Roles
- Roles and subordinates

Hands-on - Scheduling a report

We would like to schedule a report to be sent to a group of users every Friday afternoon. We need to perform the following steps:

1. Open a report, except than a joined report.

2. If you have the **Schedule Reports** permission, you should see an arrow next to the **Run Report** button. Click on the arrow and then click on **Schedule Future Runs....**

3. On the **Schedule Report** page, specify a running user and ensure that this user has access to the folder where the report is stored.

4. The user specified as the running user determines the report results generated. In this exercise, select **John Smith.** as the user.

 You need the **View All Data** permission to specify a running user other than yourself.

5. Set the recipients. We will select a public group existing in our organization. Otherwise, you can select the **To me** option so that the report will be delivered only to you.

6. The **Schedule Report** frequency when set as **Weekly** recurs on **Friday**.

7. Set the **Start** and **End** date values.

8. Choose the available time from **Preferred Start Time**.

9. Click on **Save Report Schedule** to save the schedule.

When a Salesforce user becomes inactive, scheduled reports that are configured with that user as a running user will not run. The system administrator will receive an e-mail notification from Salesforce. The options available are as follows: activate the user, delete the report schedule, or change the running user to an active user.

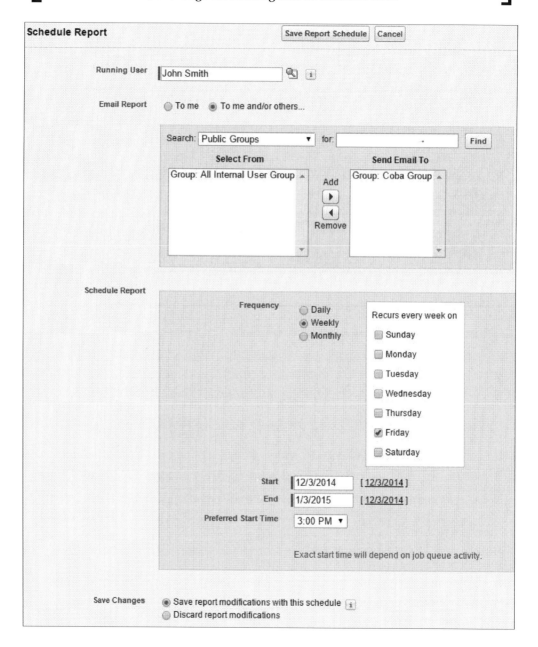

Seeing which reports are scheduled

You can easily check whether or not a report has been scheduled when you click on the **Reports** tab. Notice a column with a date and time icon in the header. A report with a tick mark on this column means that it is scheduled. You can click on the icon to sort so that all reports scheduled will be seen at the top. Only users with the **Schedule Reports** permission can see the icon.

But imagine you have many report folders. This means you need to go through each folder to identify the reports being scheduled. Another way is to look for **Schedule Jobs**. It will show all the reports scheduled by all the users:

1. Navigate to **Setup | Jobs | Scheduled Jobs**.
2. Look for items with **Type** as **Report Run**.
3. To make it easier, you can create a view for all jobs and filter it with **Type** as **Report Run**.

This view will show all the reports scheduled with the following information when the report schedule is submitted, when it was first started, and when the next scheduled run is.

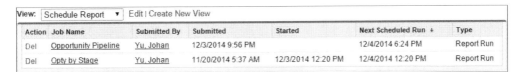

Managing a scheduled report

Managing a scheduled report is common as your business changes; you will need to change or even unschedule a report. Earlier, you learned how to identify the reports that are scheduled.

To change anything related to the scheduled report, open the report from the **Reports** tab, or from the **Scheduled Jobs** view. Click on the arrow next to **Run Report** and then click on **Schedule Future Runs...**. This is the same as what is done when you create a schedule for a report. In the **Schedule Report** window, you can modify a running user, e-mail recipients, and frequency.

If you want to stop the schedule for the report, go to the **Schedule Report** window in the preceding section and click on the **Unschedule Report** button. This button is visible only if the report is scheduled. Once the report is unscheduled, it will be removed from **Scheduled Jobs**, but it will still be available in the existing report folder.

Limitations

The last topic that we will discuss in scheduling reports is the limitations you may face. Like many other areas in Salesforce, there are always limitations based on your Salesforce edition. All the limitations are stated according to the current releases; this may change in future.

You can schedule up to 200 reports, and there is also an hourly limit as follows:

- For Professional and Enterprise editions, up to one per hour
- For Performance and Unlimited editions, up to two per hour

This is why you may not see every single hour available for you to select when you click on **Preferred Start Time**.

If you need to schedule more reports, reach out to your Salesforce account executive.

Adding an embedded report chart

Wouldn't it be nice if you could present a graphical chart of opportunities for an account in the account page layout? An embedded chart is a great out-of-the-box Salesforce feature that is used to embed a report charts in standard or custom object pages.

Instead of showing all records, an embedded report chart allows us to filter only the records related to the parent record in the page layout; for example, in the account page, only opportunities related to that account are displayed. By looking at such a chart, the user will easily understand the pipeline and all the opportunities related to the account.

The following screenshot shows an example of an embedded chart:

A few points to note related to an embedded report charts are as follows:

- You can only add up to two report charts to a page layout
- The chart shown is based on the chart added in the summary or matrix report
- You cannot modify the chart types in the page layout
- You can set the chart to auto-refresh when users open the page layout
- When users click on the chart in the page layout, Salesforce will open the report and auto add filtering based on the parent record of the report where the user opens the record

Hands-on - adding report charts to the page layout

In this exercise, we would like to add an embedded chart of all opportunities, and another embedded chart to show cases related to that account in the account page layout. You need to perform the following steps:

1. Create opportunity reports that group by stage, add amount, Amount, summarize it, and add a vertical bar chart. Save it in a public folder.

2. Create a case report that is grouped by status, and add a horizontal bar chart. Save it in a public folder.

Edit the account page layout by navigating to **Customize | Account | Page Layouts**. Open the correspondence page layout and look for **Report Charts** in the menu to the left. Click on **Report Charts** and find the reports in the panel to the right. Only reports that are publically available and have a chart will be shown.

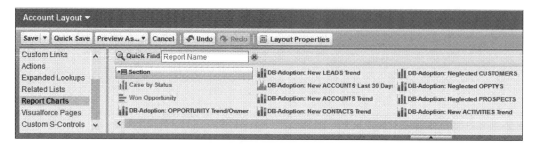

3. You will see the chart type as an icon for the report.

4. Drag both the reports created into the report area. You can create a new section if necessary.

5. Once the component is added to the page layout, click on the properties to modify the following details:

   ◦ **Size: Small, Medium**, and **Large**

   ◦ **Appearance: Show title from report, Hide chart from error**

○ **Data**: Filter and refresh

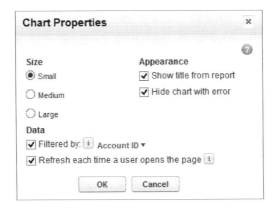

6. Filter is the most important item, as this item is used to determine the data shown in the chart. For both the reports, select **Filtered by: Account ID**.

7. Enable both **Show title from report** and **Hide chart with error**.

8. Tick **Refresh each time a user opens the page**. Otherwise, it will refresh every 24 hours.

9. Click on the **Save** button.

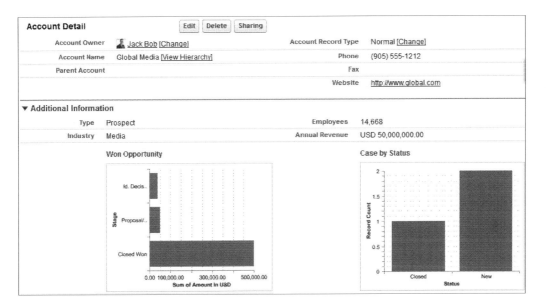

If the user does not have access to the report and **Hide chart with error** is enabled, the user will see a blank area in the page layout. If it is not enabled, the user will see an error message, as shown in the following screenshot:

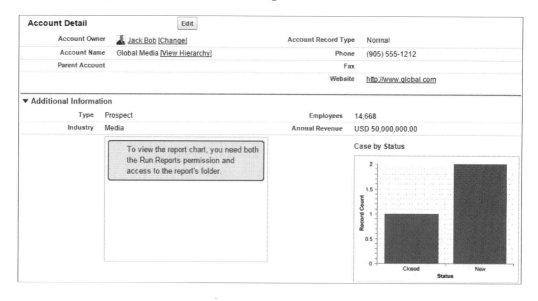

If you do not tick **Refresh each time a user opens the page** for the chart, the user will see a **Refresh** button and the time the last refresh was performed.

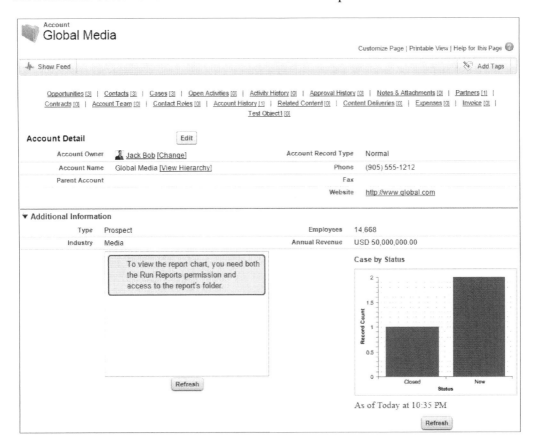

Notice the **Refresh** button shown below the chart and the information about when the last refresh performed.

Summary

This chapter concluded the reporting section of this book. We started by creating bucket fields with multiple types of field sources. The way to define the bucket values is different for each field type. We then continued with using the custom summary formula to calculate the total amount based on numerical values in the report, including the powerful formulas of `ParentGroupVal()` and `PrevGroupVal()`. These are only available in the custom summary formula.

The last two topics discussed were on scheduling a report to send reports in HTML format to your own account or to multiple users. Configuring report schedules is a very simple task in Salesforce, with just a few clicks. Finally, we discussed how to create a chart that is added to the report into a page layout so that users can get a snapshot of a record.

In the next chapter, we will start discussing dashboard in Salesforce, starting with components used to build a dashboard, followed by how a report is related to the dashboard. We will conclude with collaboration between the dashboard and Chatter.

6
Creating Your First Dashboard

From *Chapter 3*, *Creating Your First Report*, to *Chapter 5*, *Learning Advanced Report Configuration*, we discussed Salesforce reports in general. Moving forward, in this chapter, you will learn the basics of dashboards in Salesforce, and continue to *Chapter 7*, *Learning Advanced Dashboard Configuration*, to learn the advanced features of dashboards in Salesforce.

In Salesforce, the concept of a dashboard is based on reports. Each dashboard can contain up to 20 components, and each component relate to a report, which serves as the data source. You can use a report as the data source for multiple dashboard components, for example, for different graphical presentations or in different dashboards. But each dashboard component can use only one report as the data source.

In this chapter, we will create a dashboard from scratch, but before creating a dashboard, let's cover permissions and components related to dashboards. We will continue with enabling dashboards for the Chatter feed; with this, user will be able to collaborate with other users in the dashboard feed. Once a dashboard is created and stored in a public folder, other users can follow it, take a snapshot, and post it on a group feed.

The following topics will be covered in this chapter:

- Dashboard permissions
- Dashboard folders and permissions
- Defining a Salesforce dashboard
- Dashboard components
- Creating your first dashboard
- Collaborating dashboards with Chatter

Dashboard permissions

Before we start to create the dashboard, let's discuss permissions related to the ability of a user to view, create, and edit dashboards in Salesforce.

Run Reports

We discussed the **Run Reports** permission in *Chapter 3, Creating Your First Report*. We are not going to repeat that, but here, we would like to emphasize that a dashboard in Salesforce is based on reports. Each dashboard component in Salesforce is supported by a report as the backend data source.

To allow other users to view the dashboard, the user needs the permission to run reports and be able to access the report used as a data source for a dashboard component.

Without the **Run Reports** permission, the user will get the **Insufficient Privileges** error after clicking on the **Dashboard** tab. The same happens in the **Home** tab; the dashboard section will be blank when the user does not have this permission.

Run Reports is a basic permission for the user to work with reports and dashboards, including just as a viewer.

Create and Customize Dashboards

The **Create and Customize Dashboards** permission controls the user's ability to create new dashboards or modify existing dashboards. Without this permission, the user will not see the **New Dashboard...** button when they click on the **Reports** tab.

This permission requires the **Run Reports** permission. If the **Run Reports** permission is disabled for a user, enabling the **Create and Customize Dashboards** permission is useless.

Manage Dynamic Dashboards

The **Manage Dynamic Dashboards** permission allows a user to create and edit dynamic dashboards. We will look at dynamic dashboards in more detail in *Chapter 7, Learning Advanced Dashboard Configuration*. With dynamic dashboards, users are allowed to change the dashboard-viewing user to a logged-in user, or select other users based on the user permissions.

When creating or editing a dashboard, the user with this permission will have the option to set **Dashboard Running User**, as shown in the following screenshot:

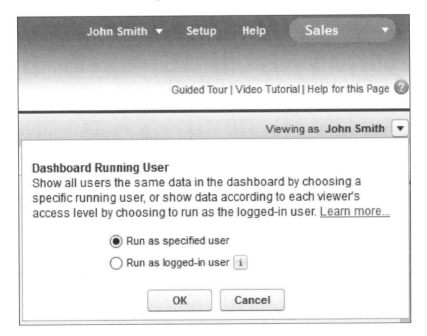

View My Team's Dashboards

The **View My Team's Dashboards** permission allows the user to view dashboards owned by people under them in the role hierarchy.

When creating or editing dashboards, users with the **Manage Dynamic Dashboards** permission and **View My Team's Dashboards** permission have the option to set the **Dashboard Running User**, and to enable **Let authorized users change running user**, as shown in this screenshot:

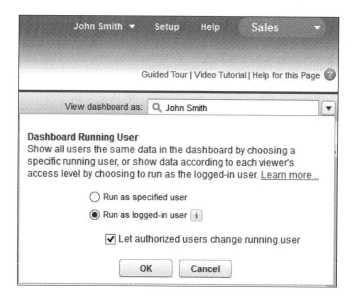

When viewing a dynamic dashboard, the user with the **View My Team's Dashboards** permission is able to enter the name of the user under them in the role hierarchy as the viewing user.

On the other hand, users with the **View All Data** permission are able to enter any other user as the viewing user, as shown in the following screenshot:

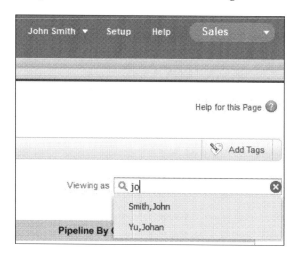

Dashboard folders and permissions

Similar to reports, every dashboard is stored in a folder, which is called the dashboard folder. You cannot store reports in a dashboard folder, nor can you store dashboards in a report folder. We will look into permissions related to the dashboard folder later in this chapter.

In *Chapter 3, Creating Your First Report*, we discussed reports and the report folder. The same applies to dashboards. A few notes on dashboard folders and permissions are as follows:

- Each dashboard is stored in a dashboard folder, not in a report folder. It can be a public dashboard folder or your private folder, called My Personal Dashboards.

- You can easily differentiate between a report folder and a dashboard folder by looking at the folder icon, as shown in the following screenshot:

- Depending on the user permission and folder permission, Salesforce will determine the folder's visibility and accessibility to a user, and determine the user having read-only or read-write accessibility.

- When a folder is visible to a user, the user will be able to see and open all dashboards stored in that particular folder, as long as the user has read access to the reports and data used as data source for the dashboard components.

Create Dashboard Folders

The **Create Dashboard Folders** permission gives users the ability to create new dashboard folders. The **Create and Customize Dashboards** permission is required to enable this permission. When this permission is enabled, by clicking on the **Reports** tab, the user will see a folder icon next to the **All Folders** area. Click on the folder icon and you can select the **New Dashboard Folder** menu. You just need to provide a label in the **Dashboard Folder Label** textbox to create a dashboard folder.

 A dashboard folder is available in the **Reports** tab. To create a new dashboard, you need to start from the **Reports** tab, while editing and opening a dashboard can be done from either the **Dashboards** or the **Reports** tab.

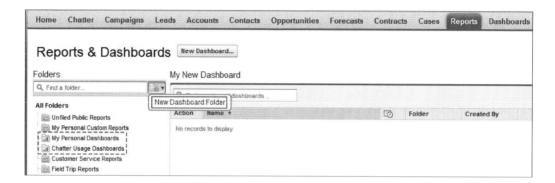

Notice that in the left panel in the preceding screenshot, you can easily distinguish between the report folder and the dashboard folder by the folder icon.

Edit My Dashboards

You may remember the **Edit My Reports** permission in *Chapter 3, Creating Your First Report*. **Edit My Dashboards** is a similar kind of permission. It allows the user to edit, move, save, and delete dashboards you created in public dashboard folders.

When a user has access to a folder, the user is able to save dashboards to that folder, even though the user's accessibility to that folder is only **Viewer**. Users are also able to edit and delete reports created by them in the public dashboard folder where they have the **Viewer** access.

This permission is not supposed to be given to any end user, as it allows them to overwrite dashboards created by others, even though the access given to that dashboard folder is only **Viewer**.

View Dashboards in Public Folders

The **View Dashboards in Public Folders** permission gives the user visibility and access to *all* the dashboards stored in public dashboard folders, although the user is not listed in the sharing access for that particular dashboard folder.

Like the **Edit My Dashboards** permission, this permission is also not supposed to be given to a normal end user.

Manage Dashboards in Public Folders

The **Manage Dashboards in Public Folders** permission requires the **Create Dashboard Folders**, **View Dashboards in Public Folders**, and **Edit My Dashboards** permissions. With this permission, users are able to access and edit *all* the dashboards stored in public dashboard folders.

On top of that, this permission allows users to share, edit, and delete any public dashboard folder. So, this is a very powerful permission.

 Be careful to give this permission only to users who absolutely need it. Make sure that users with this permission will not mess up the dashboards created by other users.

Hands-on – creating a dashboard folder

Let's create a dashboard folder with the following steps:

1. Navigate to the **Dashboards** tab.
2. Click on the **New Dashboard Folder** option under the folder icon.

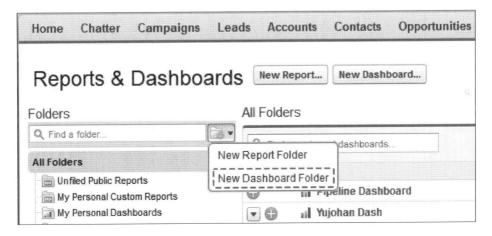

3. Enter `My First Dashboard Folder` in the **Dashboard Folder Label** textbox.

4. Click on the **Save** button. The folder created will be shown in the **All Folders** area in the left panel in the **Reports** tab.

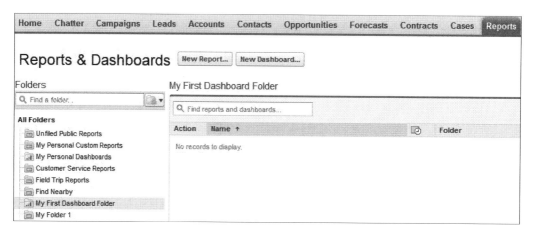

Looking at the preceding screenshot, let's analyze the available dashboard folders:

- The **My Personal Dashboards** folder is a secure dashboard folder used to store your personal dashboards. No one can access the reports inside this folder; even your system administrator cannot access them. For dashboards stored in this folder, since it's accessible only by you, you may store the reports used as the data source in the **My Personal Custom Reports** folder.

- **My First Dashboard Folder** is a standard public dashboard folder that you just created in the preceding steps. You will automatically have the **Manager** access to the folder you create. Users with the **View Dashboard in Public Folders** permission are able to access all the dashboards in any public dashboard folder, even though they are not added to the folder sharing list for that dashboard folder.

Viewing dashboards

A dashboard is a visualization of Salesforce data based on criteria in reports. You can use a mixture of charts, tables, or matrices as dashboard components. A dashboard visualizes data stored in Salesforce and helps you to identify trends, sort quantities, and measure the impact of their activities.

We can view a dashboard in two areas in Salesforce:

- The **Dashboards** tab
- The **Home** tab

The Dashboards tab

The **Dashboards** tab is a special tab in Salesforce. When you click on the **Dashboards** tab, you will be presented with the last dashboard you opened. The system will also capture your last five dashboards opened and add them in order in the top section, that is, **Recently Viewed**.

Once the dashboard page opens, you can find other dashboards by typing or scrolling down in the **Find a dashboard...** dropdown. Each dashboard will be put under its dashboard folder name.

The Home tab

The **Home** tab is the most common page in Salesforce. By default, when a user log in to Salesforce, they will land in the **Home** tab. So, adding dashboard components to the **Home** tab is a good idea, if you have a dashboard that all your users should see. The system administrator can configure to add dashboard component in the **Home** layout for all or particular users based on the user profiles.

Dashboard components will be seen in the top row of a dashboard on the home page. Users can select which dashboard to see. The following screenshot shows the **Home** tab:

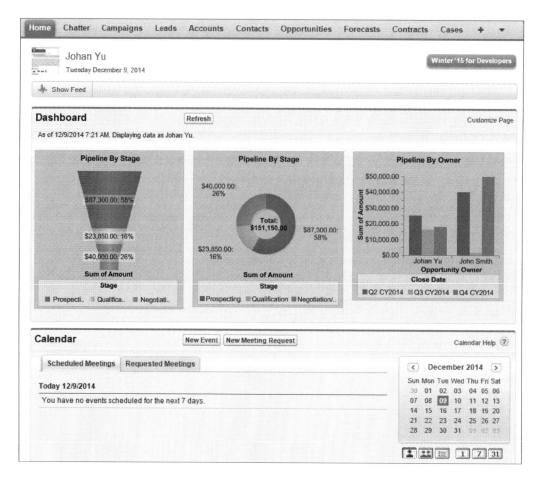

In the **Home** tab, a user can select a dashboard they prefer to see in their **Home** tab, but only the top row components from the dashboard selected will be shown in the **Home** tab.

Data shown in the dashboard will be based on a user set as a **Viewing** user, whether it is you or someone else. You can see the **As of ....** and **Displaying data as ....** labels in the preceding screenshot of dashboard components, for the last refresh and the viewing user.

Click on the **Refresh** button here to refresh the dashboard with the latest data in Salesforce. Once a dashboard has been refreshed, other users who open the same dashboard will see dashboards based on the latest refresh by another user.

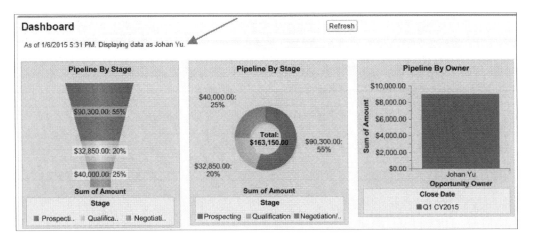

Selecting a dashboard for the home page

If users have access to more than one dashboard, they are able to select the dashboard they would like to see in their **Home** tab. When users log out and log in again, they will see the dashboard selected by the user in the **Home** tab.

When the selected dashboard is a dynamic dashboard, it will show the current user as the viewing user, and there is no option to select another user as the viewing user in the **Home** tab.

To select a dashboard for the **Home** tab, perform the following steps:

1. In the **Home** tab, click on the **Customize Page** link to the right in the dashboard component.
2. It will bring the user to **Customize your Home Page**. Select a dashboard from the available dashboards in the **Show Data From:** section.

3. The user will see all the dashboards that they have access to. The list of the dashboards is based on dashboard folder sharing and user/profile permissions.

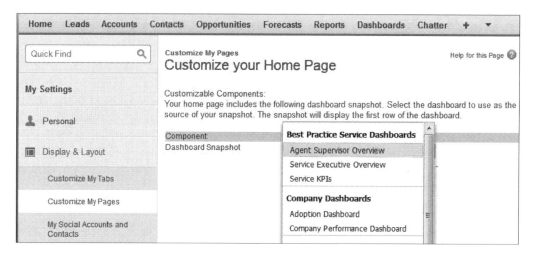

Dashboard components

A user can access dashboards from the **Dashboards** tab, depending on the dashboard folder permissions and user permissions. One dashboard can contain up to 20 components. Each component can be present in the form of a chart, table, or matrix. On top of that, you can also select the Visualforce page component type.

We will not discuss the Visualforce page as a component in detail in this book; this is just additional information. When standard components that are provided out of the box do not fit your requirements, use Visualforce page is an option.

The two main steps to build a dashboard are as follows:

1. Select the component.
2. Select the data source.

Components

There are seven types of charts supported by Salesforce dashboards:

* Horizontal bar chart
* Vertical bar chart

- Line chart
- Pie chart
- Donut chart
- Funnel chart
- Scatter chart

In addition to charts, you can choose metric and table as component types. The following screenshot shows the different components available:

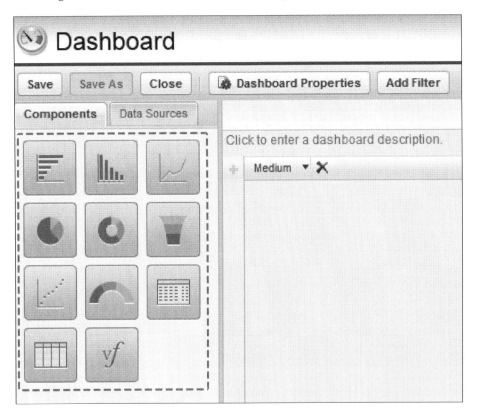

Data sources

Salesforce gives you the flexibility to use any saved reports as data sources. However, components that use reports saved in `My Personal Custom Reports` will not work for other users; only you can access the dashboard.

You can use any report type as a data source, with exceptions:

- **Tabular report**: Only tabular reports with a limited **Row Count** filter and configured dashboard settings can be used as data sources. Choose a name and value to use in the dashboard tables and charts. Tables show both the name and the value. Charts are grouped by name.
- **Joined report**: Only joined reports containing charts in the report can be used as data sources. You must select **Use chart as defined in source report**.

Each dashboard component needs a report acting as a data source for the component. But for the Visualforce page component, instead of selecting a report, you need to provide a Visualforce page as a data source.

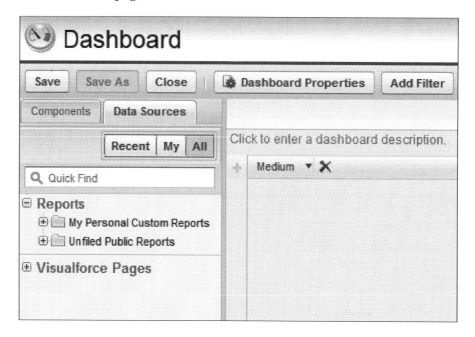

If the report used as a data source contains a chart, you can use the report's chart in the dashboard component. Select **Use chart as defined in source report** in the dashboard component settings. Enabling this option will disable selection of the chart type for the component, and it will always follow the chart type added in the report. Remember that in reports, we can add charts with the following types:

- Horizontal bar chart
- Vertical bar chart
- Line chart

- Pie chart
- Donut chart
- Funnel chart

Defining a dashboard component

We will not discuss each type of chart in this book, but you need to understand a few items when defining a dashboard component. In both **Component Editor** of the dashboard component and **Chart Editor**, when you add charts to the report, you have two tabs to configure the settings:

- **Component Data**
- **Format**

Component Data

Component Data in dashboards has options similar to those of the **Chart Data** tab in report charts.

The options available in this tab depend on the type selected; for example, for a bar chart, you can define **Y-Axis**, **X-Axis**, **Group By**, and **Combination Charts**. Compared to the same bar chart in the report's **Chart Editor** window, you have two additional options for the dashboard: **Display Units** and **Drill Down to**. These two options are available in all types of dashboard component editors, but not in the report chart editors.

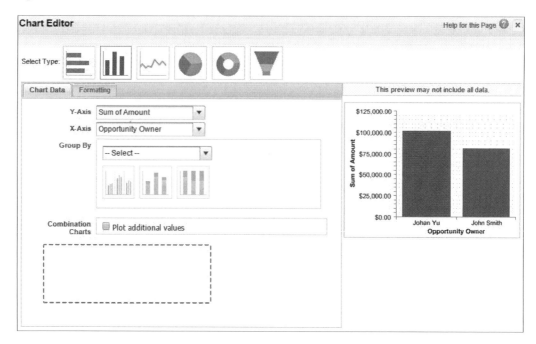

The preceding screenshot is taken from a report's **Chart Editor** window. Note that it does not have the **Display Units** and **Drill Down to** options, unlike the dashboard's **Component Editor**.

Formatting

Similar to the **Component Data** tab, the options available in the **Formatting** tab also depend on the chart type. But compared to **Chart Editor** in reports, the selection available in the **Formatting** tab in the dashboard's **Component Editor** window is lot different; only **Show Values** and **Show Details on Hover** are the same.

For example, in a bar chart, you can define **Sort Rows By**, **Maximum Values Displayed**, **Axis Range**, **Legend Position**, and **Data Labels**. These values are not available in the report's **Chart Editor** window, but there are also many options available in the report chart editor that do not exist in the component dashboard.

Here is a screenshot of the **Formatting** tab from the dashboard's **Component Editor** window:

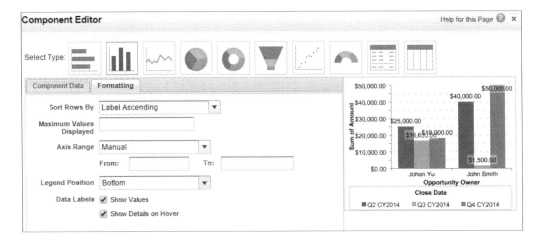

Let's take a look at the **Formatting** tab for the same bar chart in a report's **Chart Editor** window:

The takeaway from this section is that we should not assume that options and features of charts are the same in reports and dashboards.

Creating your first dashboard

We have discussed many topics in this chapter related to creating a dashboard, which include the following:

- Dashboard permissions
- Report folders and permissions
- Defining a Salesforce dashboard
- Dashboard components

Well, now let's start creating a dashboard.

Hands-on – creating a dashboard

Let's create a dashboard with a component showing the number of accounts per sales representative in a vertical bar chart:

1. Navigate to the **Reports** tab.

> If you do not see the **Reports** tab, click on the + icon in the last tab to see all the available tabs. If you still cannot find it, contact your system administrator.

   You will be presented with the available report and dashboard folders in the left panel, and the recently viewed reports and dashboards in the main area.

2. A report is the basic need for dashboards, as it is used as a data source for a dashboard component, so let's create the report first:

   1. Click on the **New Report...** button.
   2. Select the **Accounts** report type under the **Accounts & Contacts** category.
   3. Click on the **Create** button to continue.
   4. Select **All accounts** in the **Show** filter.
   5. Change the **Create Date** range to **All Time**.
   6. Change the report format to **Summary**.
   7. Remove all columns and add only **Account Name** to the report.
   8. Drag **Account Owner** onto the grouping drop zones.
   9. Navigate to **Show | Details** to hide the record details.

10. Save the report as `Account by Owner` in a public report folder.

3. Navigate to the **Reports** tab again and click on the **New Dashboard...** button.

4. By default, you will see the **Components** tab open in the left panel and three columns or dashboard components with medium width.

5. Drag the horizontal bar chart into the dashboard area, and drop it into the first column (to the left).

6. Change the column width to **Wide**.

7. Click on the **Data Sources** tab.

8. Select the report we just created, that is, the **Account by Owner** report. Click on the + sign for the reports, and click on + again for the report folder. Click on the report name and drag it into the report component added. Alternatively, type the report name in the textbox; the system will show reports containing the name as you type. Then drag the report into the component added.

9. Edit the component title as `Account by Sales Rep`.

10. Click on the **Save** button, enter the dashboard name as `My Dashboard`, and save it in the `My First Dashboard Folder` folder created earlier. Click on the **Save and Run Dashboard** button to see our first dashboard.

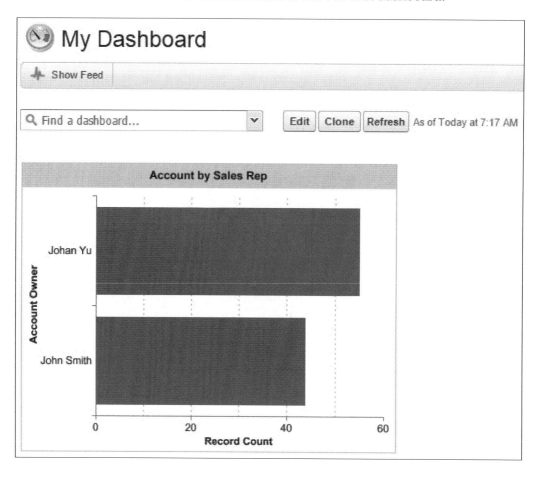

Let's continue by adding another dashboard component:

1. Click on the **Edit** button.
2. Drag a pie chart into the central column.
3. Find the same report, **Account by Owner**, and drag it into the pie chart component.
4. Enter Account by Sales Rep in the component title.
5. Click on the **Save** button and then on the **Close** button to continue.

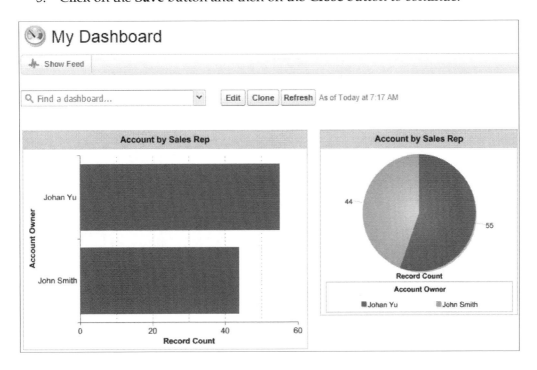

Let's modify some settings for the preceding pie chart:

1. Click on the **Edit** button.

2. Click on the tool icon (edit attributes) for the pie chart.

   This will open **Component Editor** for the pie chart.

3. In the **Formatting** tab, select **Show %** and unselect **Show Values**.

4. Click on **OK**, **Save**, and then **Close** to continue. The following screenshot shows how the dashboard looks after this change is done:

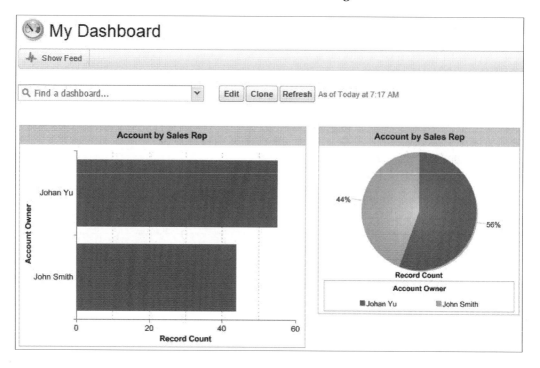

You can add up to 20 components in a dashboard.

Remember that to create a dashboard, we start from the **Reports** tab and click on the **New Dashboard...** button. Once you save and open the dashboard, it will be shown in the **Dashboards** tab. Dashboard creation is not started from the **Dashboards** tab.

Hands-on – editing and maintaining dashboards

There are two ways to edit a dashboard:

- **The Reports tab**: Find the dashboard and click on the **Edit** link from the drop-down arrow.

- **The Dashboard tab**: Find the dashboard and click on the **Edit** button. You can type the dashboard name in the **Find a dashboard...** textbox; it will filter the available dashboards based on the text you type in that box.

 If you do not see the **Edit** button after opening a dashboard, this means you do not have permission to edit the dashboard, whether because of the folder sharing access or **Dynamic Dashboard** permission.

Once you are in the **Edit** mode, you can add, delete, or modify existing components when you create a new dashboard. You save the modified dashboards as new dashboards by clicking on the **Save As** button.

While viewing a dashboard, you can clone the dashboard by clicking on the **Clone** button. The far right button when opening dashboards is the **Refresh** button. Click on this button to refresh the dashboard using the latest data in Salesforce. The next user who opens the same dashboard will see charts based on the data you refreshed. The information on when dashboard refresh is available can be found next to the **Refresh** button.

Integrating dashboards with Chatter

In a report, you can track the report name and description changes in the Chatter feed. The same applies to a dashboard; you can track a dashboard in the Chatter feed for:

- Dashboard Running user
- Dashboard unique name
- Description
- Title

Additionally, in a dashboard, you can post a dashboard component as a snapshot to:

- The Chatter dashboard feed
- The Chatter group or user feed

Feed tracking

You can utilize the Chatter feed in a dashboard to collaborate with your team, for example, to draw attention to the sales pipeline and so on.

Let's open **My Dashboard**, which we created earlier. Below the dashboard name, there is a panel and a link called **Show Feed**. Clicking on this link will display **Post**, **File**, **Link**, and **More**, as shown in the following screenshot. The feed here is the same as the Chatter feed in other objects, such as **Account**, **Opportunity**, and so on. You can get other users' attention by using @ followed by the username. Ensure that the user has access to the dashboard, otherwise this will be useless.

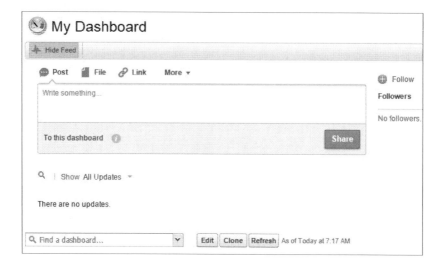

Notice a round **+** button in green and the **Follow** label; this is also the same as in other objects such as **Account, Opportunity**, and so on. Click on this icon to follow the dashboard. You will be notified about the changes to the dashboard for items it tracks: running user, description, name, and title.

If you do not see this, ensure that the dashboard is enabled for **Feed Tracking**. To validate this, you can perform the following steps:

1. Navigate to **Setup | Customize | Chatter | Feed Tracking**. Look for **Dashboard** and tick **Enable Feed Tracking**.

2. There are four fields available for tracking here: **Dashboard Running User, Dashboard Unique Name, Description**, and **Title**.

When you click on the **Reports** tab, notice the same round **+** button with a green icon or the blue tickmark icon before the dashboard name. You can click on the former button to follow the dashboard, while the latter button means that you have followed that dashboard.

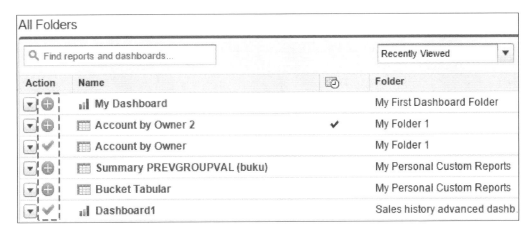

Posting a dashboard snapshot

To enable a dashboard snapshot, navigate to **Setup | Customize | Reports & Dashboards** and look for **Enable Dashboard Component Snapshots**.

A snapshot post is a static image from a dashboard component at the time it is posted. If the dashboard has a filter applied, the snapshot image will be based on the components with that filter. Information on when the snapshot was posted and the viewing user will be added to the snapshot post.

There are two options for posting dashboard snapshots: to a dashboard feed and to a user or group feed.

When a snapshot is posted on a dashboard feed, all users who are able to access the dashboard will see a snapshot of the dashboard at a point in time. To post a snapshot on a dashboard feed, perform the following steps:

1. Open the dashboard.
2. Hover your mouse over the component; notice the arrow that appears in the top-right corner of the component.
3. Click on the arrow and select **Post Snapshot to Dashboard Feed**.
4. Enter a comment for the snapshot; this is required.

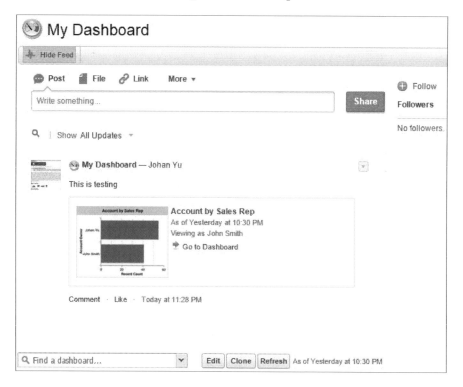

Posting a snapshot to a Chatter group will get the attention of other users in the Chatter group. Snapshots posted to the Chatter group feeds can be seen by everyone in that group, even by those without access to the dashboard, so don't post sensitive information. To post a snapshot to a Chatter group, follow these steps:

1. Open the dashboard.
2. Hover your mouse over the component; notice the arrow that appears in the top-right corner of the component.

3. Click on the arrow and select **Post Snapshot to User or Group Feed**.

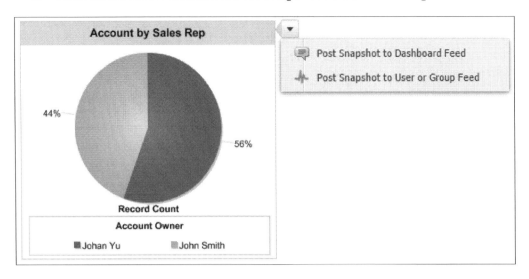

4. Select the **Group Feed** tab and enter a Chatter group name and comment for the snapshot; both of these details are required.

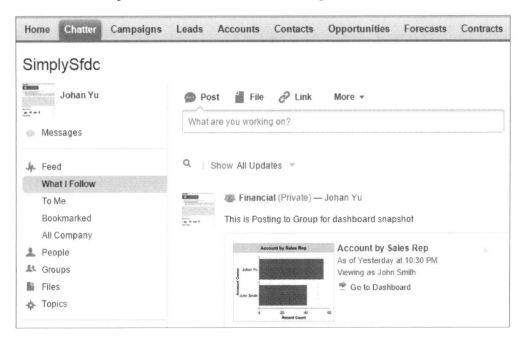

Summary

We started this chapter with permissions related to dashboards, and then continued with dashboard folders and the permissions related to a dashboard folder. Next, we discussed the definition of a Salesforce dashboard and how it is created.

A dashboard component is an important area in building dashboards in Salesforce. Finally, we created a dashboard from scratch by modifying some attributes and using a few types of charts.

We concluded this chapter with how to relate dashboards to Chatter for collaboration with other users, using the Chatter feed, and posting snapshots to a feed, a Chatter group, or a user feed.

In the next chapter, we will continue with dashboards. We will discuss advanced configuration of dashboards, including how to manipulate the dashboard component results using dashboard filters and dynamic dashboards.

7
Learning Advanced Dashboard Configuration

In *Chapter 6, Creating Your First Dashboard*, we discussed basic dashboard creation, starting with various permissions related to the dashboard and dashboard folder. You learned the basic structure of a dashboard, how it is related to the report, and where it is defined and stored in the Salesforce platform. We continued with the dashboard component, which is the heart and soul of dashboards in Salesforce. Finally, we created a dashboard from scratch, enhanced it, and utilized Chatter to share the dashboard with your team.

In this chapter, you will continue to learn and create advanced dashboards using out-of-the-box functions offered by Salesforce. We will start with the dashboard filter, how to implement it, and other use cases for the dashboard filter. We will continue with the concept of dynamic dashboards, which was discussed in *Chapter 6, Creating Your First Dashboard*. Finally, we will look at the dashboard drill-down in Salesforce and look for prebuilt dashboards available at AppExchange.

The following topics will be covered in this chapter:

- Implementing dashboard filters
- Using dynamic dashboards
- Dashboard and report drill-down
- Getting more from AppExchange

Implementing dashboard filters

Have you ever had the need to analyze a dashboard based on different criteria? For example, we would like to look at the pipeline dashboard for the current year, current quarter, and current month.

For this example, it is not an issue to create three dashboards, but since the data source of dashboard is driven by reports, it means that we would need to create three sets of reports for each dashboard. If you have 10 components for the dashboard, you will need 30 reports to support it.

Therefore, instead of creating multiple dashboards, it would be useful if we could have only one dashboard, since all the components for the dashboard are the same. Also consider the maintenance effort required for 30 reports and three dashboards, compared to one dashboard with 10 reports used as the data source.

Dashboard filter comes into the picture for these requirements. With just one dashboard, you can change the filter to include different records in the dashboard based on the selected filter.

Definition and concept

Dashboard filter is a great feature for filtering the data used in the dashboard component. All components will be filtered according to the filters selected. With the dashboard filter, you can use the same dashboard to provide different combinations of data.

When you apply dashboard filter, all data sources for components in the dashboard must be reports. This means you cannot use a Visualforce page as the data source in any of the components for dashboard while applying a filter.

When you select filters on a dashboard, the last filter will be selected by default when you open the dashboard again.

To create a dashboard filter, you have to define a label for the filter, select a field that contains the type of information you want to filter, and then define how the filter returns the data. Each filter ideally contains more than one value, including the operator. You can have a maximum of 10 values, and each dashboard can have up to three filters.

Hands-on – adding a filter to a dashboard

Let's use My Dashboard created in *Chapter 6, Creating Your First Dashboard*. We will add a filter based on **Account Creation Date** with option equal to **This Month**, **This Quarter**, and **This Year**. This allows users to analyze the number of accounts created over a year, a quarter, and months:

1. Open and edit the dashboard. If you are navigating from the **Reports** tab, you can directly click on the **Edit** link. It is located under the arrow in the **Action** menu:

2. Click on the **Add Filter** button:

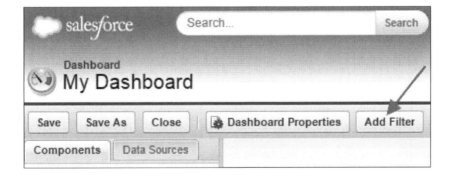

3. Select the field you would like to use as a filter. In this exercise, select **Created Date**.

4. In **Display Label**, type **Account Creation Date**.

5. In **Filter Options**, select **Operator** as **equals**. You can leave the **Group Name** value blank or enter a `Current Month` label to represent the value. For **Value**, type `THIS MONTH`.

6. Click on **Add Row** and repeat the preceding steps for `THIS QUARTER` and `THIS YEAR`. The following screenshot shows the updated values:

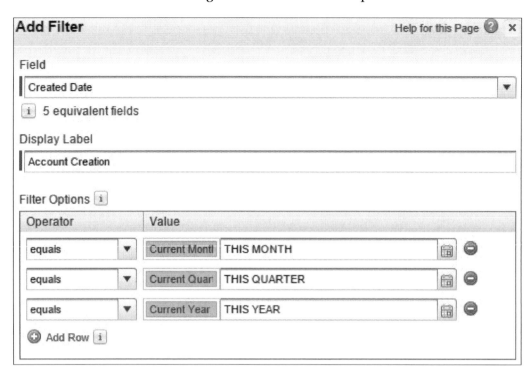

7. Click on the **OK** button, **Save** button, and then **Close** button to continue.

You should see the dashboard added with a filter, as shown in this screenshot:

To remove or edit the filter, click on the **Edit** button in the dashboard and look for the **Edit Filter** and **Remove Filter** links in the filter dropdown:

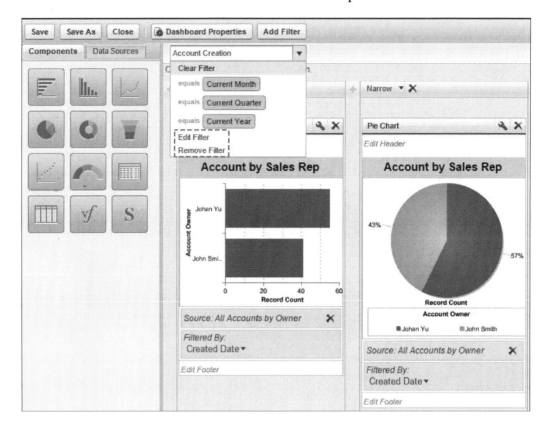

 You can have up to three filters in a dashboard. To add more filters, click on the **Add Filter** button in the dashboard edit mode.

Using a dynamic dashboard

Before we start with the definition of dynamic dashboards, let's understand: is there any concept called a static dashboard? Yes, there is, but it is not called a "static dashboard". For simplicity in this book and to differentiate a dashboard from a dynamic dashboard, let's just call it a "normal" dashboard. Note that in Salesforce, it is officially just called dashboard, not "normal dashboard".

Normal dashboard

For a normal dashboard, the user will see a dashboard with data visibility of someone else. Let's take a sample of how data visibility works in a normal dashboard. We create a role hierarchy to explain this easily, as shown in the following diagram:

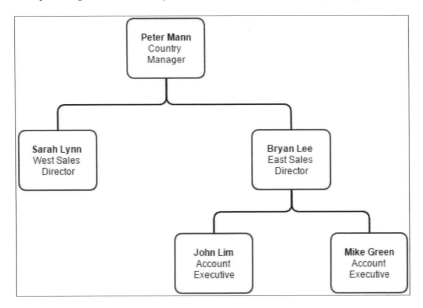

Let's say a normal dashboard is configured with a running user as Peter Mann. Any user who opens the dashboard will have data visibility as that of Peter Mann, even though the user does not have visibility of the records, or even the source report used as a dashboard component.

When you create or edit a normal dashboard, select **Run as specified user**, as shown in the following screenshot. The dashboard runs using the security settings of that single, specific user. All users with access to the dashboard see the same data, regardless of their personal security settings.

When a user clicks on the dashboard component, it will show data visible for login user, not dashboard running user.

One of the good use cases for using a normal dashboard is to show the dashboard with Viewing user as someone from top-level management in the company, such as the business unit head or country head, so all employee knows the overall company performance. Another use case to use this dashboard is to show each team performance; this will motivate team member's performance to compete with other teams.

What is a dynamic dashboard?

So, what is a dynamic dashboard in Salesforce? Dynamic dashboards offer users the ability to run a dashboard with data based on the running user's data visibility, or data visibility of someone in your team or your organization, depending on the user permissions. With a dynamic dashboard, you can control data visibility without having to create a separate dashboard, with its own running user and folder for each level of data access.

In *Chapter 6, Creating Your First Dashboard*, we discussed permissions related to dashboards. Some of them are specifically related to dynamic dashboards only:

- **Manage Dynamic Dashboards**
- **View My Team's Dashboards**

Users with the **Manage Dynamic Dashboards** permission are able to create and edit dynamic dashboards. A dynamic dashboard is marked with **Run as logged-in user** selected, so each user will see different data in the dashboard based on their data visibility. This is different from a normal dashboard when all users see the same data, based on one person's data visibility only.

When users with the **View My Team's Dashboards** permission open a dynamic dashboard with **Let authorized users change running user** selected, users are able to select another user under their team from the role hierarchy. So all of the data in the dashboard will be refreshed with the visibility of that user. This includes user data, the data shared with them, and the data under that user's team. Furthermore, users with the **View All Data** permission will be able to select any user in the dynamic dashboard.

Limitations

The number of dynamic dashboards you can configure depends on your Salesforce edition; you can have up to five dynamic dashboards for Enterprise Edition, 10 dynamic dashboards for Unlimited and Performance Editions, and three for Developer Edition. For additional dynamic dashboards, you can contact your Salesforce Account Executive to acquired more dynamic dashboards.

You can't save a dynamic dashboard in a personal folder. Dynamic dashboards must have shared access. You also cannot schedule a dynamic dashboard. Dynamic dashboards need to be refreshed manually.

Hands-on – creating a dynamic dashboard

Let's consider the following use case: we want to change a normal dashboard to a dynamic dashboard and let the user choose the running user in the dashboard.

Before you start, make sure you have the **Manage Dynamic Dashboards** and **View My Team's Dashboards** permissions. Otherwise, you will not see the **Dashboard Running User** selection. You can reach out to your Salesforce administrator if you do not have these permissions. They are defined in your user profile setup, or can be individually added to your user details using **Permission Set**.

Again, let's use My Dashboard for this exercise and make sure it is not a dynamic dashboard.

Before we change the dashboard to a dynamic dashboard, let's look at the dashboard again. Notice that the viewing user of the dashboard is **Johan Yu**. The following screenshot was taken when logged in as **John Smith**:

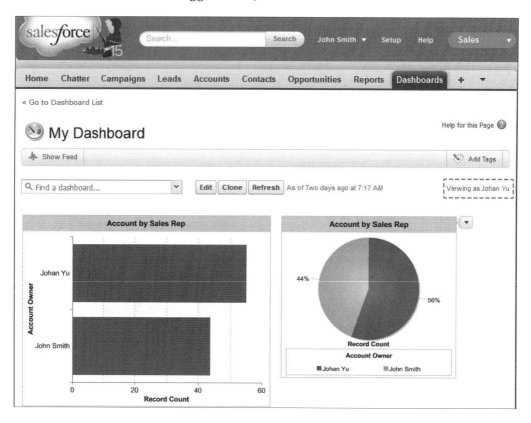

We perform the following steps to change the dashboard:

1. Navigate to the **Reports** tab, search for the dashboard, and click on the **Edit** link under the arrow before the dashboard name. Alternatively, you can edit the dashboard from the **Dashboards** tab and click on the **Edit** button.

2. In the top-right corner, look for **View dashboard as**. It should show a username.

3. Click on the arrow to the right of the textbox.

4. Change the selected value from **Run as specified user** to **Run as logged-in user**. This selection causes the dashboard to become a dynamic dashboard.

5. Enable **Let authorized users change running user**. This option allows users with the **View My Team's Dashboards** and **View All Data** permissions to run the dashboard as someone else's view, depending on user permissions and role hierarchy.

6. Click on the **OK** button to continue and then on the **Save** and **Close** buttons, as shown in the following screenshot:

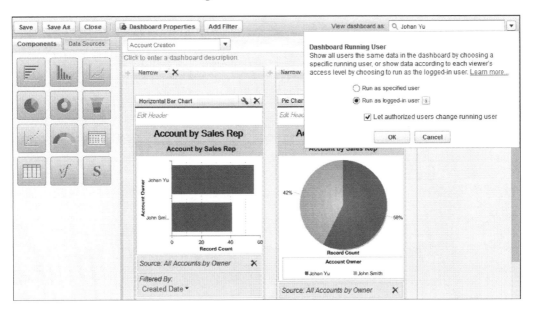

Let's see the dashboard after it has been configured as a dynamic dashboard. The viewing user is now **John Smith**, who is the user logged in to Salesforce, instead of **Johan Yu** was the default viewing user before we converted the dashboard. Also, the values in the chart are changed based on the visibility of **John Smith**. The updated values are shown in the following screenshot:

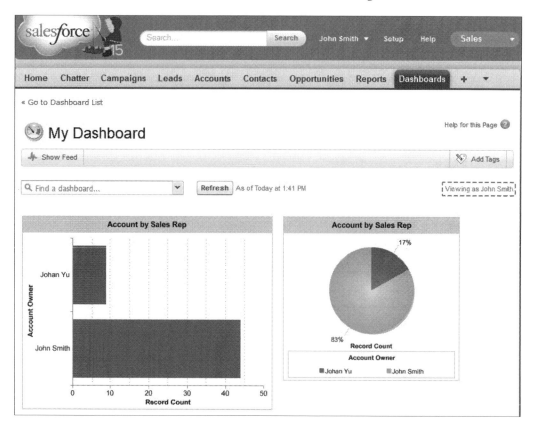

Dashboard and report drill-down

As we discussed in *Chapter 6, Creating Your First Dashboard*, a dashboard is built on components, and each component has a report or a Visualforce page as the data source. Components that use the Visualforce page as the data source will display the Visualforce page itself, not the normal component type available for dashboard. When user clicks on the component, action will depend on the logic that has been built on that Visualforce page.

For components that use reports as data sources, when a user clicks on the component, it will take them to another page, either to the source report or somewhere else. As an administrator, you can define the following page type selection so as to show when the user clicked on the component:

- **Source Report**
- **Filtered Source Report**
- **Record Detail Page**
- **Other URL**

For most dashboard components, the drill-down value will have an option for all four selections, as you just saw. For the table component, however, **Filtered Source Report** is not available. For a gauge component in a matrix report, only **Source Report** and **Other URL** are available.

To configure this selection, edit the dashboard and click on the tool icon in the component:

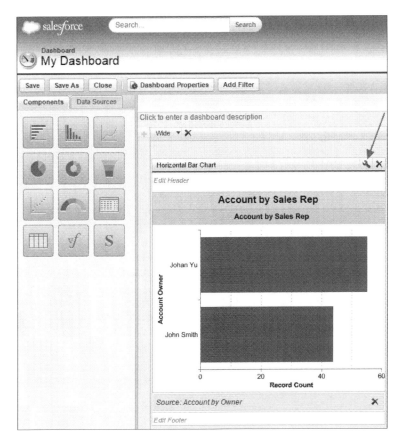

Once **Component Editor** is open, the **Component Data** tab will be selected by default. Select a value in **Drill Down to**:

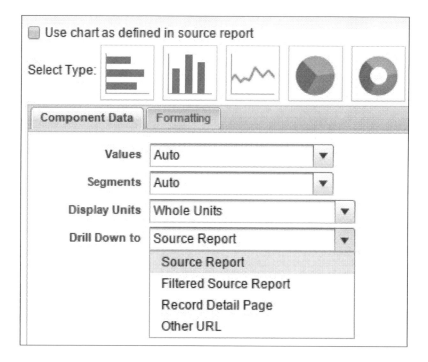

Source Report

The **Source Report** option is the default selection when you create a component using report as the data source. When you open the dashboard and click on the component with this selection, it will take you to the full report used as the data source.

For a normal dashboard, when user clicks on a dashboard component, data shown in the report is data visible to login user, not data visible by user defined as dashboard's Viewing user. The user will see **Note: You ran this report by clicking a dashboard component. Results may differ from the dashboard due to your security settings in the report.**.

You can easily notice the drill-down to **Source Report** by hovering your mouse over the component. It will show a **Click to go to full report** help text.

Filtered Source Report

The **Filtered Source Report** option is more advanced than **Source Report**. It will detect where users click on the chart. When a user clicks on a group in the chart, they will be taken to the source report, filtered by what they clicked on. Let's look at an example:

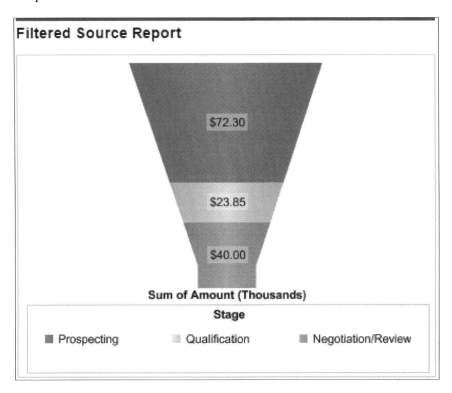

When users click on the **Qualification** group in the chart, they will obtain the source report, with the **Stage equals Qualification** criteria added to the report:

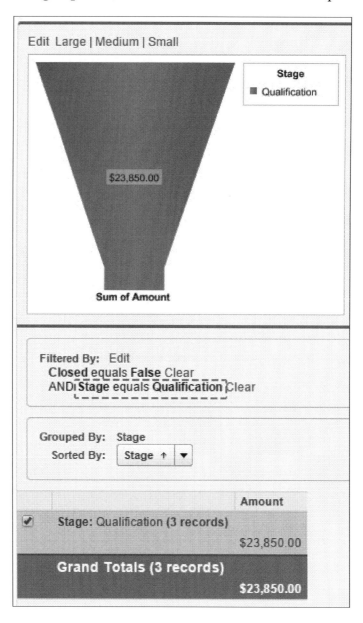

The **Stage equals Qualification** filter is not defined in the original source report. It is temporarily added when the user clicks on the **Qualification** area in the chart of the dashboard component.

This option is not available in gauge, metric, and table component types.

When you open the dashboard, for a component with **Show Details on Hover** enabled, you can easily notice the drill-down to the settings. Hover your mouse over the component, and it will show a **Click to go to filtered report** help text.

Record Detail Page

When you select the **Drill Down to** value as **Record Detail Page**, it will bring you to the details page for that record, depending on the area clicked on.

This option is available for the table component, and also valid for charts that use a source report grouped by record name, record owner, or feed post only. However, the source report is not grouped by picklist value, bucket field, and so on. Remember that the report has to be grouped by a physical record, for example, **Account by Owner**:

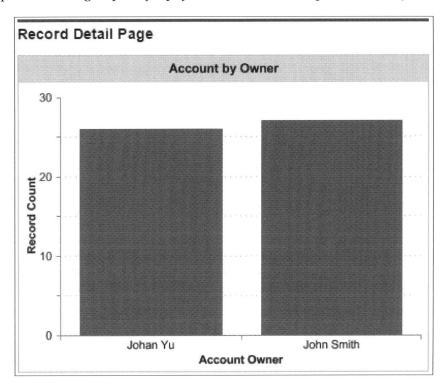

When you click on the **Johan Yu** bar, it will take you to the user details page, not the source report:

Let's look at another sample of a dashboard component using table. The report used as the data source for this component is the `Opportunity Summary` report, with sum of **Amount** and grouped by **Name**:

Top 10 Opportunity	
Opportunity Name	Sum of Amount
Baru Phase-II	$25K
Hello Part-2	$21K
Jayabaya 2 Mph	$19K
Baru Phase-I	$18K
Drill in Sub-Ocean	$18K
Hello Part-1	$17K
Qaa-II	$10K
Hello Part-3	$10K
Jakarta-Stage 2	$9K
New Datapipe	$7K

Like the table component, clicking on any opportunity name will open the opportunity details page, not the source report.

Other URL

When you create a dashboard component and select **Drill Down to** as **Other URL**, you will be prompted to enter a URL in Salesforce or outside Salesforce. When the user clicks on the component, it will take them to the specified URL. For URLs outside Salesforce, remember to add `http://` or `https://`; for example, if you enter just `www.yahoo.com`, it will become `https://ap1.salesforce.com/www.yahoo.com`, which is invalid. Here, `ap1` is your Salesforce instance name.

If you do not enter any URL in the textbox in dashboard configuration, the **Drill Down to** option will be automatically set back to **Source Report**.

Report drill-down

For the dashboard component with **Drill Down to** as **Source Report** or **Filtered Source Report**, when users click on the component, it will take them to the source report. If the report is a summary or matrix report, user can drill down to it.

The same applies if a user manually opens a summary or matrix report, they will notice a checkbox to the left of the report:

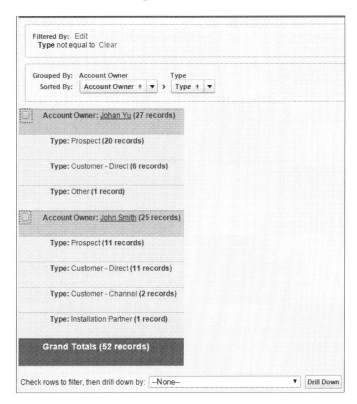

Notice the checkboxes in the summary report or the matrix report, as shown in the following screenshot:

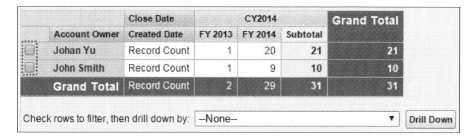

		Close Date	CY2014			Grand Total
	Account Owner	Created Date	FY 2013	FY 2014	Subtotal	
☐	Johan Yu	Record Count	1	20	21	21
☐	John Smith	Record Count	1	9	10	10
	Grand Total	Record Count	2	29	31	31

Check rows to filter, then drill down by: --None-- ▼ [Drill Down]

If you scroll to the bottom, you will see **Check rows to filter, then drill down by:**. You can select a field available in the dropdown for drill-down and then click on the **Drill Down** button.

Selecting the checkboxes

For the summary report, if you select **Johan Yu** and then click on the **Drill Down** button without selecting any field, the report will be filtered to show only the account owned by Johan Yu, by including an additional filter in it:

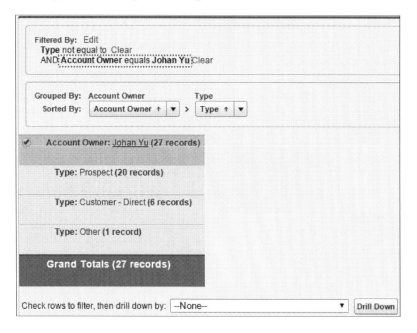

If you select more than one checkbox, all the selected values in the group will be added to the report filter. The same applies to the matrix report.

Selecting a field

What happens when you select a field from the dropdown at the bottom, but do not select any grouping checkbox, and click on the **Drill Down** button? The following screenshot shows a summary report group by **Account Owner**, then **Type**; user selects the **Industry** field from the drop-down menu and clicks on **Drill Down**.

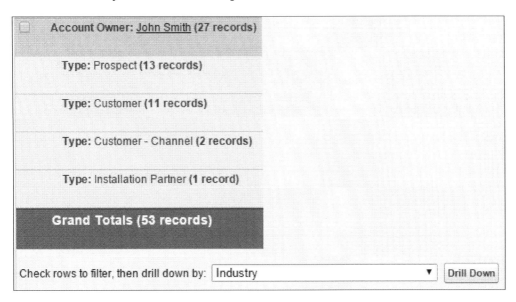

For summary format report, this will change the first level grouping, while for matrix report, it will change the grouping for the first row grouping.

Here is a screenshot showing a sample of the result. Notice that the **Account Owner** grouping changed to **Industry** when you selected **Industry** for drill-down, as shown in the following screenshot:

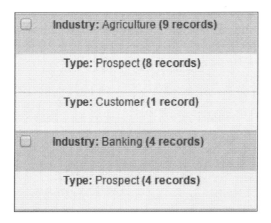

Combining checkboxes and fields

In previous section, first we selected a group to drill down, then we selected a field without selecting the group to drill down. Now, we would like to combine both to drill down.

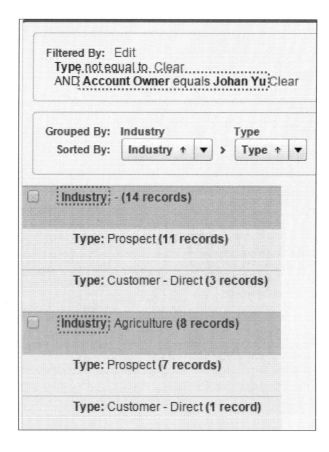

Notice that additional filter criteria are included based on the checkbox selection, and at the same time, the first level grouping changes to **Industry**. We select the **Industry** field in the drop-down value before clicking on **Drill Down**:

1. Adding report filter with values from selected checkboxes.

2. Change the first level grouping for the report.

Getting more from AppExchange

If you are not familiar with AppExchange, let me explain, AppExchange is a business app store hosted by Salesforce.com for Salesforce users. Here, you can find thousands of apps can be installed on your Salesforce instance to meet or enhance your business needs. Some of the apps are free, while many have a license fee. They are built by Salesforce partners. In addition, there are some sample apps provided by Salesforce Labs. Salesforce Labs does not support the apps it posts on the AppExchange, but offers many examples of Salesforce features that help administrators learn how to use those features.

An app installed from AppExchange is considered a third-party app, which means it is not supported by Salesforce. For paid apps, the developer will usually provide support.

To reach Salesforce AppExchange, go to `https://appexchange.salesforce.com`. You will see many apps there, or you can search by entering a keyword in the search textbox.

To find an app related to the dashboard, type `dashboard` in the search textbox. You will get many dashboard apps built by Salesforce Labs, which you can install and use for free, and from Salesforce partners. It is good practice to always try in a Sandbox before deploying an app on the production environment. For the app you installed from AppExchange, you can choose to uninstall it without causing any problems for the rest of your Salesforce organization.

A few dashboard apps built by Salesforce Labs are as follows:

- Salesforce CRM Dashboards
- Sales Activity Dashboard
- Chatter Usage Dashboards
- Salesforce1 Adoption Dashboard and Reports

As you know, a dashboard is supported by reports behind the scenes, so when you install any of these apps, it will include the reports needed as the data source. If the standard presentations of dashboards or data filters or groupings do not match your organization, you can easily modify and save them as new reports and dashboards. The following screenshot shows the apps available on AppExchange:

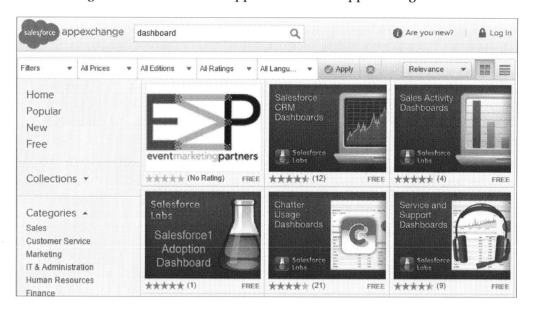

Summary

This chapter concluded the topic of dashboards. We started with implementing a dashboard filter so that a dashboard can be used for multiple scenarios, instead of creating a dashboard for each criterion.

We continued with a deep dive into dynamic dashboards. You learned how they are different from normal dashboards, how to create dynamic dashboards, and the limitations of using dynamic dashboards.

We concluded with drill-down options in the dashboard component into reports used as source data, including drill down to filtered source report. Furthermore, we discussed report drilldowns by fields and by selected groups. Finally, we explored how to get prebuilt dashboards from AppExchange, whether they are free or paid.

In the next chapter, we will discuss how to access historical data and the setup required for that. We will cover a few options on how to access historical data and the limitations for each option.

8
Accessing Historical Data

Salesforce reporting uses live Salesforce data when producing reports, while dashboards show data based on the latest dashboard refresh—either manual or scheduled. In *Chapter 2, Managing Data in Salesforce.com*, we discussed how to back up data in CSV files with weekly data exports or using the AppExchange product, and how to build your own custom sync application with local database.

In this chapter, we will discuss various options for accessing historical data in Salesforce, but without using backup data, which we discussed in *Chapter 2, Managing Data in Salesforce.com*. We will start with field history tracking, where you can track the changed field values, what the values were before and after, and who changed it and when. Then, we will continue with Chatter feed tracking for collaboration, and reporting snapshots, which is used to store a snapshot of data in a custom object. Historical trend reporting is the latest feature added to Salesforce out of the box. It highlights changes between snapshot dates, such as days, weeks, and months.

Each of these options has strengths and limitations, and we will cover them in this chapter. The following topics will be covered in this chapter:

- Setting and using field **History Tracking**
- Implementing Chatter **Feed Tracking**
- Implementing **Reporting Snapshot**
- Implementing **Historical Trending** in reports

Setting up and using field History Tracking

Tracking field history is an out-of-the-box Salesforce feature to track value changes in a field. You can define up to 20 fields per object to track. Contact Salesforce support if you need to track more fields. For a long text area, rich text area, and multi-select picklist fields, Salesforce does not track the old and new values when the record is updated, but only track a change has occurred for the field. This feature is simple but powerful for auditing purposes.

Salesforce will retain the data history for up to 18 months. If you need to archive for longer periods, contact Salesforce support to acquire the Field Audit Trail feature and define a policy for the time you wish to retain field history tracking. This payable feature will allow you to extend archiving for up to 10 years.

As an administrator, you can enable field history tracking yourself with a few clicks, and select certain important fields to track for both standard and custom objects.

Remember with field tracking, the field value is not tracked until the object is enabled for tracking, and the fields are selected. This means that if you just enable tracking for the account name, you cannot use field tracking to track the account name before the time you enable field tracking on account name.

History tracking does not only mean tracking when you edit a record; it also includes the time you create new records, including the records created from lead conversion. The field history entry will be **Created** when you create a new record, and **Created by lead convert** when it is converted from **Lead**. Both the old value and the new value will be blank.

History tracking on standard objects

History tracking supports both standard and custom objects, but not all standard objects are supported by field tracking. Only the following objects are supported: **Account, Contact, Lead, Opportunity, Case, Contracts, Entitlements, Service contracts, Contract line items, Articles, Solutions, Orders, Product**, and **PriceBooks**.

Field tracking is not enabled by default; to enable history tracking on a standard object, we can consider an example for the **Account** object with the following steps:

1. Navigate to **Setup | Customize | Accounts | Fields** and click on the **Set History Tracking** button.
2. Select the **Enable Account History** checkbox.

3. Select the fields you want to track.

4. Notice that **Description** will be tracked for changes only. This is because **Description** is a long text area field; the same happens if you have any other long text area or rich text area and multi-select picklist fields.

5. Click on the **Save** button to save the changes.

History tracking on custom objects

For a custom object, you need to enable it in the object details before selecting fields to track. Let's say we have a custom object named **Claim**. We need to perform the following steps for history tracking:

1. Navigate to **Setup | Create | Objects**.

2. Click on the **Claim** object link and then on the **Edit** button.

3. Enable **Track Field History** in the optional features.

4. Notice that the **Set History Tracking** button is now available in **Custom Fields & Relationships**, as shown in this screenshot:

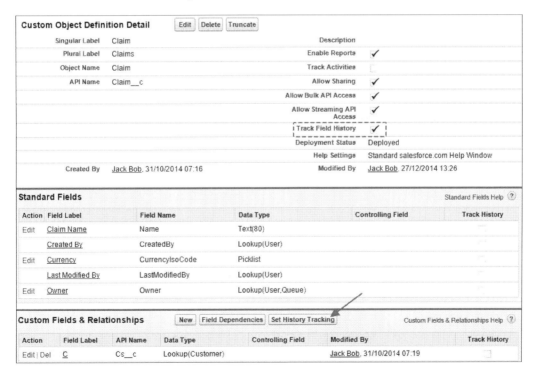

5. Click on the **Set History Tracking** button and select the fields you want to track.

6. The same steps can be done with standard objects for long text area, rich text area, and multi-select picklist fields; it will track for changes only, not the old and new values.

7. Click on the **Save** button to save the changes.

History objects

When you enable **Track Field History** for an object, at the backend, Salesforce will create a new object. That object's name will end with **History**, for example, **AccountHistory**, **ContactHistory**, and so on for standard objects. For custom objects, it will be of this type: **__History**. An example of this is **Claim__History**.

When any changes occur in a tracked field in a record, Salesforce will create a new record in this object. Suppose, for example, you have five tracked fields in an object and three of them change in one transaction. Then, Salesforce will create three records in this object.

This is for developers or admins familiar with **Salesforce Object Query Language (SOQL)**; you can look into the object to query for the following:

- `CreatedById`: This is the user who makes the change
- `CreatedDate`: This is the time of the change
- `OldValue`: This is the old value
- `NewValue`: This is the new value
- `ParentId` (for custom objects): This is the record ID related to the changes
- `ObjectId`: This is the object ID for standard objects, for example, **AccountId** or **ContactId**

You cannot create, update, or delete records in this object manually; you can only query.

For a good reason, until the Spring 2015 release, the storage usage for history objects was not counted as data storage.

Reading the history tracking value

Once you enable history tracking, there are two ways to see the tracking value, not including using the API query as in the preceding section. The two ways are discussed in the following sections.

History-related lists

You can add field-history-information-related lists to the object page layout. This information will be visible to all users that access that particular page layout, just in case you have a multiple-page layout.

To add a history-related list to the object page layout, open the page layout editor. In this exercise, let's consider the **Account** object, so the related list for this will be **Account History**. Select **Account History** in **Related Lists** and drag it onto the page layout.

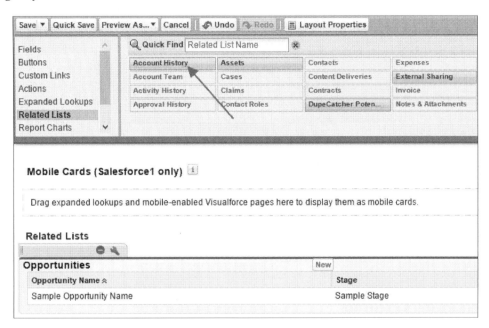

Once the history-related list is added to the page layout, any update to the fields tracked will be shown there.

Account History			
Date	User	Connection	Action
27/12/2014 16:29	Novida Lunardi		Deleted 5002 in **Account Number**.
27/12/2014 16:29	Novida Lunardi		Changed **Industry** to **Engineering**.
			Changed **Account Number** from 5001 to **5002**.
27/12/2014 16:28	Novida Lunardi		Changed **Description**.
27/12/2014 16:28	Novida Lunardi		Changed **Account Number** to **5001**.
27/12/2014 16:28	Johan Yu		Changed **Account Owner** from Johan Yu to **Novida Lunardi**
27/12/2014 16:27	Johan Yu		Created.

Let's analyze the preceding screenshot:

- It is sorted by the date and the time the change happened at in descending order.

- The first entry shows when the record is created.

- For updates to more than one field in one transaction, the updates will be tracked as two different items, but with the same date and time. See changes in **Industry** and **Account Number** for an example of this.

- If the original value is blank, it will just say **Changed Account Number to ....** When it changes back to blank, it will say **Deleted ...** in **Account Number**.

- Because **Description** is a long text area field, it will not track old and new values, but just track a change.

All objects will have the same label. It ends with **History**, for example, **Account History**, **Contact History**, **Claim History**, and so on. But for **Opportunity**, it is called **Opportunity Field History**. This is because **Opportunity History** is used for **Stage History**.

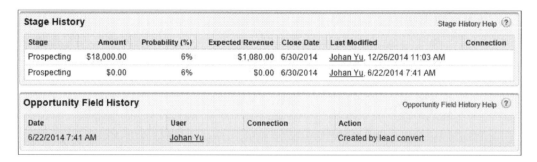

The same applies to the API object name. It will be called `OpportunityFieldHistory` instead of `OpportunityHistory`, as it is used to store **Opportunity Stage** information.

History reports

Another option to get history tracking values is by using the history report. For this, users only need the **Run Reports** permission and the permission to access the object.

For standard reports, such as **Account**, perform these steps:

1. Click on the **Account** tab and scroll down to **Account History Report**.

2. If you have the **Create and Customize Reports** permission, you can modify **Summarize Information**, **Show**, and **Time Frame**.

Another option is to create a custom **Account History Report**.

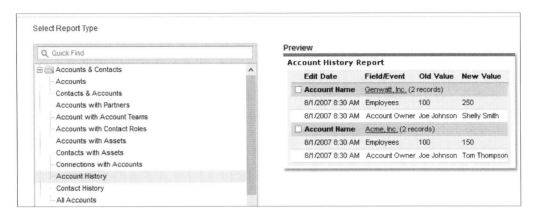

By default, it will show my accounts, but you can modify it as if it were a normal report. This includes add filter, add grouping, change report format, and add/ remove field from report. If you look at the left panel for field availability, you'll notice that only the **History Data** group will contain historical data, while other fields will show live data in Salesforce, provided you bring that field into the report.

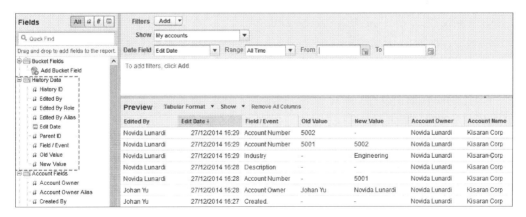

Notice in the preceding screenshot that the parent ID for the **Account History Report** type is **Account ID**. This nomenclature will be the same for other standard objects; for example, for **Contact History**, the parent ID will be **Contact ID**.

For custom objects, once you enable **Track Field History** in the object details, when creating a new custom report, you will notice that the report type ending with **History** is available for you to use, such as **Claim History**. The same applies to **Account History**. You can use this report type as a normal report.

Edited By	Edit Date ↓	Field / Event	Old Value	New Value	Claim: Owner Name
Johan Yu	27/12/2014 14:02	Account	Star Disc	-	Novida Lunardi
Novida Lunardi	27/12/2014 14:01	Description	-	-	Novida Lunardi
Novida Lunardi	27/12/2014 13:59	Account	Global Media	Star Disc	Novida Lunardi
Johan Yu	27/12/2014 13:58	Owner	Jack Bob	Maria Ann	Novida Lunardi
Johan Yu	27/12/2014 13:56	Account	-	Global Media	Novida Lunardi
Johan Yu	27/12/2014 13:56	Description	-	-	Novida Lunardi
Johan Yu	27/12/2014 13:49	Claim Name	Hello 1	Hello 2	Novida Lunardi
Johan Yu	27/12/2014 13:47	Created.	-	-	Novida Lunardi
Grand Totals (8 records)					

Limitations of using field History Tracking

Some of the limitations of using field history tracking have been explained before, but let's summarize here:

- There can be at most 20 fields to track
- For long text area, rich text area, and multi-select picklist fields, you cannot track old and new values
- Not all standard objects can be tracked, for example, **User**, **Task**, **Event**, **Campaign**, and **Quote**
- Not all fields can be tracked, for example, formula, roll-up summary, and auto-number fields, as well as all the **Created By**, **Last Modified By**, and **Expected Revenue** fields on **Opportunity**

Implementing Chatter Feed Tracking

Chatter feed tracking is similar to field history tracking, but they are not related at all. When a user follows a record tracked by a Chatter feed, any changes to the fields tracked will be seen on the user's Chatter feed, an example of which is shown here:

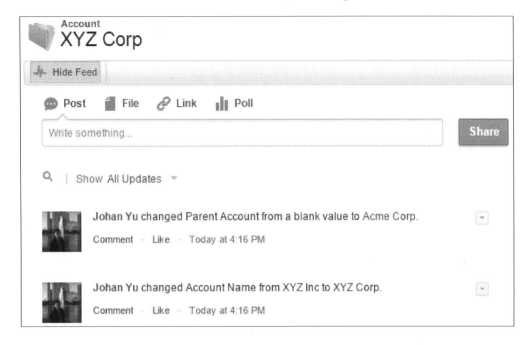

As they are Chatter feeds, other users can add comments, like them, bookmark them, and add topics on those feeds as per normal Chatter feeds.

Enabling Chatter feed tracking

Like field history tracking, enabling Chatter feed tracking is only for system administrators. There is no difference between standard and custom objects here. Perform the following steps to enable Chatter feed tracking:

1. Navigate to **Setup | Customize | Chatter | Feed Tracking**.
2. Select the object, for example, **Account**.
3. Tick **Enable Feed Tracking**.
4. Select the fields you want to track—up to 20 fields.
5. Click on the **Save** button to continue.

The same with field history tracking, for long text area, rich text area, and multi-select picklist fields, it does not track the old and new values when a record is updated; it only notes that a change has occurred.

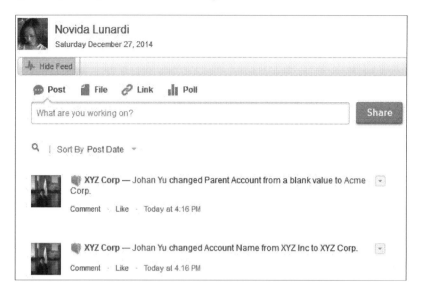

In Chatter feed tracking, the admin can also enable display feed activity for related objects, as long as Chatter feed tracking is enabled for the related objects. Let's see a sample showing how this works:

In **Account** feed tracking, we can enable tracking all the related objects. So, when an opportunity is created for that account, opportunity fields tracked will be shown in the **Account** feed along with users who follow that account.

Feed objects

When you enable Chatter feed tracking for an object, at the backend, Salesforce will create a new object with the name of the object ending with **Feed**, for example, **AccountFeed**, **ContactFeed**, and so on for standard objects. For custom objects, it will be __**Feed**, for example, **Claim__Feed**.

When any changes occur in a tracked field in a record in one transaction, Salesforce will create only one new record in this object. For example, suppose you have five fields tracked in **Account** and two of them change in one transaction. Salesforce will create only one record for the feed. This is different from field tracking, which will create two records.

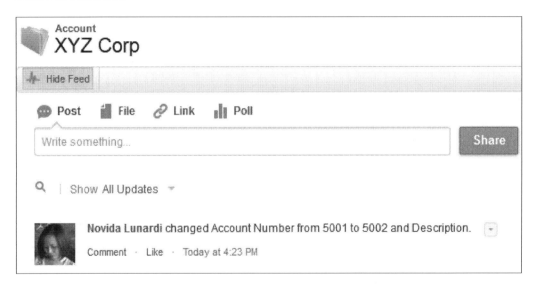

You cannot create and update records in this object manually, but users with **Modify All Data** or **Moderate Chatter** permissions are able to delete it.

Like field tracking, the storage usage for feed objects is not counted as data storage.

Implementing Reporting Snapshots

Can we have a report of data trending in Salesforce? Does Salesforce only report current data? Field history tracking will store old and new values whenever there is any change in the record value. To use it for trending will be too difficult, unless you export the data to an external database and analyze it with live data. You will need a business intelligence tool for this, which is not simple and cheap.

So is there any other way to store historical data so that we can easily use it for reporting? Yes, if you are using Salesforce Professional edition or higher editions, you can configure snapshot reporting to store historical data.

Just like field tracking, do not expect old historical data to be available before you configure the reporting snapshot. Historical data for a specific reporting snapshot will only be available after it has been configured properly and run.

Each Salesforce edition has a limited number of reporting snapshots that can be created and scheduled, so use them wisely. Alternatively, you can contact Salesforce support to acquire more number of snapshots.

Configuring Reporting Snapshots

Only a user with the **Manage Reporting Snapshots** permission is able to create and configure snapshot reporting. In summary, here are a few major steps to follow when you need to configure and implement snapshot reporting in Salesforce.

Creating the source report

First of all, create a report with the tabular or summary report format. The number of records created in the target object will depend on the number of records returned in the source report.

For a tabular report, it will be one to one, meaning each row in the report will create a record in the target object.

For a summary report, it will be by group summary or grand summary.
If you choose grand summary, it will always create only one record in the target object, while group summary will create records in target object as many as number of groups return in the report.

 The maximum number of records that can be stored is 2000 per snapshot run.

Creating the target object

You need to create a custom object as the target object to store data returned from the report. Ensure that the target object is not included in the workflow.

Creating fields in the target object

With default reporting, a snapshot will give us three pieces of information that we can capture in fields in the target object: **Reporting Snapshot Name, Reporting Snapshot Running User**, and **Execution Time**. It is good practice to create fields name in the target object with similar or represent data will be created from source report. You need to create additional custom fields to capture the data being collected in the source report.

Creating the reporting snapshot

Navigate to **Setup | Data Management | Reporting Snapshots**. Click on the **New Reporting Snapshot** button and enter the following information:

- **Reporting Snapshot Name**: This will be the job name
- **Running user**: The report result will be dependant on data visibility of this user
- **Source Report**: Select the report that was created in step 1
- **Target Object**: Select the object that was created in step 2
- **Description**: It is good practice to provide information here for future reference

Mapping fields from the source report to the target object

If your source report format is **Summary**, you need to select the grouping level. The applicable source report field will be available for each target object. It is based on the field type.

Setting the schedule

Optionally, you can enable an e-mail reporting snapshot for yourself or other users. However, it is mandatory to schedule the frequency and time at which the reporting snapshot should run. Otherwise, the reporting snapshot will not be active. Select the frequency on a daily, weekly, or monthly basis and pick an available preferred start time. The selection here is similar to scheduling reports for future runs.

Hands-on – creating a reporting snapshot

This use case is to create a trend report of **Opportunity Amount** with stages for the last four months.

Step 1 - creating the source report

We will not go through each step to create reports, as it has been covered in detail from *Chapter 3, Creating Your First Report*, to *Chapter 5, Learning Advanced Report Configuration*. For this exercise, we will create a report in **Summary** format and grouped by **Stage**, and you need to add the **Amount** column and summarize it with **Sum**. See the following screenshot and make sure you get something similar to it.

You can store the report in any folder as long as the running user is able to access the report in that folder. But as good practice, create a new report folder only for the purpose of reporting snapshots.

Let's name this report Opportunity by Stage (last 120 days).

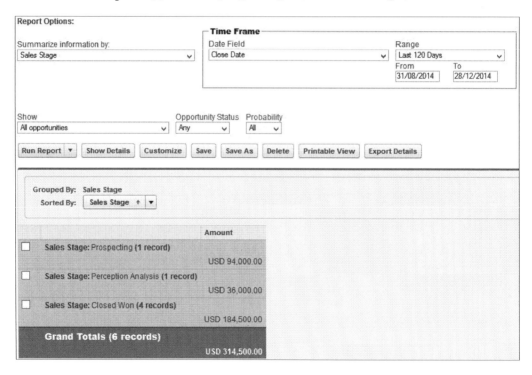

Step 2 - creating custom objects

A custom object will be used to store all values when a snapshot runs on schedule. Navigate to **Setup | Create | Objects** to create a new object. Let's name the object Opportunity Snapshot. Set the record name data type to **Auto Number**.

Step 3 - creating custom fields

From the custom object you just created, create the following fields to store values from the report and snapshot-running information, and ensure that the field created has the correct field type:

Custom Fields & Relationships		New	Field Dependencies
Action	**Field Label**	**API Name**	**Data Type**
Edit | Del	Execution Time	Execution_Time__c	Date/Time
Edit | Del	Record Count	Record_Count__c	Number(18, 0)
Edit | Del	Running User Id	Running_User_Id__c	Text(255)
Edit | Del	Snapshot Name	Snapshot_Name__c	Text(255)
Edit | Del	Stage	Stage__c	Text(20)
Edit | Del	Total Amount	Total_Amount__c	Currency(16, 2)

In this exercise, we are just capturing the group summary (this is defined by the report used as the source report, which is the summary report), so we only need a few custom fields to store the summary information. For this exercise, there is **Record Count** and **Total Amount**.

If you use a tabular report as the source report, it will capture the report details. Each column in the tabular report will be captured as a field in the target object. Each row in the report will create one record in the target snapshot object.

Step 4 - creating the reporting snapshot

This section is where we define the reporting snapshot configuration. We need to perform the following steps:

1. Navigate to **Setup | Data Management | Reporting Snapshots**.
2. Click on the **New Reporting Snapshot** button.

3. Enter the following information:

    ◦ **Reporting Snapshot Name**: Let's name this `Opportunity Trend`

    ◦ **Description**: This is optional, but it is always good practice to write a description for the snapshot

    ◦ **Running User**: This user will determine data visibility when the snapshot runs

    ◦ **Report Source Name**: Select the report we created in step 1—**Opportunity by Stage (last 120 days)**

    ◦ **Target Object**: Select the object we created in step 2—**Opportunity Snapshot**

4. Click on the **Save** button to continue.

Step 5 - mapping fields from the source report to the target object

From the reporting snapshots created, click on the **Edit** button in the **Field Mappings** section and follow these steps:

1. Select grouping level as **Grouping 1: Sales Stage**.

2. Map the summary fields from the source report to the target object.

Fields from Source Report Opportunity by Stage	Map to	Fields in Target Object Snapshot Opportunity
Execution Time	⇨	Execution Time (Date/Time)
(No fields with compatible data type)	⇨	Object Access Level (Lookup(User Record Access))
(No fields with compatible data type)	⇨	Owner (Lookup(User,Group))
Record Count [Record Count]	⇨	Record Count (Number(18, 0))
Reporting Snapshot Running User	⇨	Running User Id (Text(255))
Reporting Snapshot Name	⇨	Snapshot Name (Text(255))
Sales Stage	⇨	Stage (Text(20))
Amount [Sum]	⇨	Total Amount (Currency(16, 2))

3. Click on the **Save** button to continue.

Step 6 - scheduling reporting snapshots

From the reporting snapshots created, click on the **Edit** button in the **Schedule Reporting Snapshot** section. This is similar to what you do when you schedule a report for a future run:

- Optionally, you can enable an e-mail to be sent to you or to other users based on public groups, roles, roles and subordinates, and users.

- You can set the schedule run frequency to daily, weekly, or monthly. For this exercise, we select daily as we would like to see a daily trend.

- In the **Start Time** date, **End Time** date, and **Preferred Start Time** field, enter today's date in the start for one year with preferred time in the morning.

Summary of creating a reporting snapshot

Let's see what we have so far:

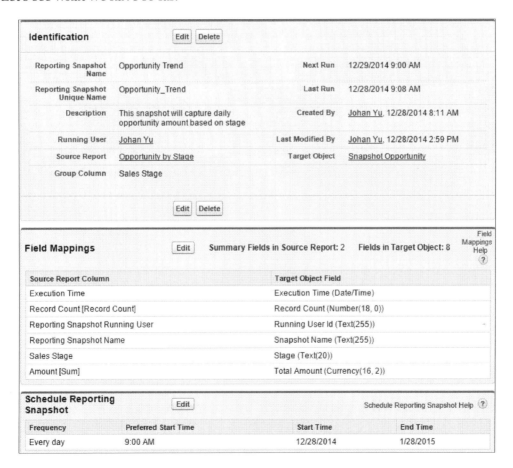

We have done all of the configuration needed to implement reporting snapshots. After this, what we can simply do is wait until we reach the preferred start time. This is a limitation, as we cannot test straightaway. However, you can run the source report manually to ensure that it is showing you the summary information you want to collect.

As we've selected **Email Reporting Snapshot** to send an e-mail to me, once the snapshot schedule finishes for the day, you will get an e-mail from Salesforce with the subject as Reporting Snapshot: {Snapshot Name} - Status - {Status}, for example, Reporting Snapshot: Open Pipeline - Status - Success. The e-mail will contain the time at which the snapshot ran, status of the snapshot run, number of records inserted into the target object, number of failure records, and a link to the reporting snapshot log. Here is a screenshot showing a sample e-mail:

The reporting snapshot Opportunity Trend ran from 12/28/2014 9:08 AM to 12/28/2014 9:08 AM. Below are details about the reporting snapshot:

2 records were inserted into the target object from the source report

0 records failed to load into the target object from the source report

The following fields on the target object could not be mapped: null

The status of the reporting snapshot is: Success

You can obtain further details by viewing the reporting snapshot's run detail page, or by clicking this link: https://cs21.salesforce.com/0A8q0000000086b. If you are not currently logged into salesforce.com, you will be asked to do so to view the reporting snapshot's run detail page.

Thank you,

salesforce.com

History and monitoring reporting snapshots

To look for a past schedule that was run for the snapshot, open a particular reporting snapshot and scroll down to the **Run History** section, just below where we schedule it in **Schedule Reporting Snapshot**.

If you have multiple reporting snapshots scheduled, you can monitor from **Scheduled Jobs**. Navigate to **Setup | Jobs | Scheduled Jobs**. Look for items with the type **Reporting Snapshot**.

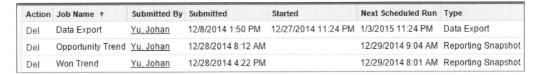

If you're an admin, this page will show you all the reporting snapshots scheduled and the time of the next scheduled run for each snapshot.

Reports on historical data

Once the snapshot runs, it will copy the report result to the target custom object. You can create a normal report to analyze data in that custom object. Just ensure that **Enable Reports** has been enabled for that custom object.

Let's see how the data is copied in the target object by creating a report:

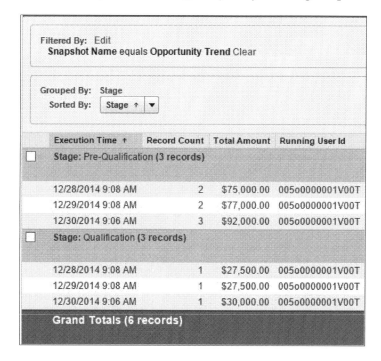

For this example, with this report, we can analyze **Record Count** and **Total Amount** by **Stage**, which changes over days.

Limitations of reporting snapshots

The following points show the limitations of reporting snapshots:

- You only have up to 100 fields in your source report. This happens particularly when you use tabular reports as the report source.
- You need to ensure that the running user is able to access the objects and fields mapped.
- When a reporting snapshot runs, at most 2,000 new records can be inserted into the target object. This also particularly happens again when you use a tabular report as the report source.
- The target object is just a normal custom object, so an admin or a user with read-write permission to the object is able to manually insert, delete, or update values. This is different from field history, in which there is read-only access for admin users.

Implementing historical trending reports

A historical report can help the sales manager monitor the team's sales pipeline to make sure they meet the current and future sales goals. You'll probably want to compare historical and current values of key attributes of opportunities that have changed over time, such as amounts and status of your team pipeline.

Historical trend reports offer this capability without any special additional permission for the user to run the historical trending report. However, the admin needs to configure the objects and fields enabled for historical trending.

The same applies to field history; the historical trend will not track the fields until you enable historical trending for the object.

Historical trending on standard and custom objects

Historical trending could be enabled on the following standard objects:

- **Opportunity**: When you enable historical trending in **Opportunity**, by default, the following fields are always enabled:
    - **Amount**
    - **Close Date**
    - **Forecast Category**
    - **Probability**
    - **Stage**

    You can add more fields to enable historical trending in **Opportunity**.

- **Case**: No fields are enabled by default.
- **Forecasting item (for collaborative forecast only)**: The following fields will always be enabled:
    - **Amount Without Adjustments**
    - **Amount Without Manager Adjustment**
    - **Quantity Without Adjustments**
    - **Quantity Without Manager Adjustment**
    - **Forecast Amount**

- ° **Forecast Quantity**
- ° **Owner Only Amount**
- ° **Owner Only Quantity**

You can manually activate any custom object for historical trending, but only up to three objects are allowed.

Hands-on – configuring historical trending

Let's consider the following use case: the management wants to analyze all the opportunities won this year. Show any changes of **Amount**, **Close Date**, and **Stage** compared to one week ago and one month ago.

Activating historical trending on Opportunity

To activate historical trending on **Opportunity**, you need to perform the following steps:

1. Navigate to **Setup | Customize | Reports & Dashboards | Historical Trending**.
2. Look for the **Opportunity** object.
3. Select **Enable Historical Trending**.
4. Click on the **Save** button, since we do not need other fields to track.

Creating a historical trending report

To create a historical trending report, perform the following steps:

1. Create a new report and select opportunities with **Historical Trending** as the report type. This special custom report type is created when your admin enables historical trending for **Opportunity**.
2. Grab all the fields as required and drop them into the **Report Builder** area.
3. Change **Time Frame** to **Current FY**.
4. Change the **Filter Stage** value to **Closed Won**.

5. There is a special filter for trending reports. It is called **Historical Field Filter**. When you click on the arrow next to the **Add** button, it will be on the top, and it will be default if you click on the **Add** button. For this exercise, enter **Stage (Historical): 1 Month Ago not equal to "Closed Won"**.

6. Another special item here is **Historical Date**. You can select up to five dates for trending reports. For this exercise, let's select **Yesterday**, **1 Week Ago**, and **1 Month Ago**.

7. Run the report and see the result.

Filtered By: Edit
Stage equals **Closed Won** Clear
AND **Stage (Historical)** 1 Month Ago not equal to **Closed Won** Clear

Historical Date: 1 Week Ago, 1 Month Ago

Account Name: Account Name	Opportunity Name	Amount	Amount (Historical)		Close Date	Close Date (Historical)		Stage	Stage (Historical)	
		Today	11/28/2014	12/21/2014	Today	11/28/2014	12/21/2014	Today	11/28/2014	12/21/2014
Maxima Inc	Max-Star X fish	$2,300.00	$2,300.00	$2,300.00	12/7/2014	11/17/2014	12/7/2014	Closed Won	Needs Analysis	Closed Won
Jakarta-1	Jakarta-14K BAS	$14,000.00	$400.00	$14,000.00	11/30/2014	7/18/2014	11/30/2014	Closed Won	Prospecting	Closed Won
Jayabaya	Key Phase-3	$23,000.00	$5,000.00	$3,000.00	11/26/2014	8/5/2014	11/26/2014	Closed Won	Prospecting	Closed Won
Semaku1	Semaku-Two day	$1,600.00	-	$1,600.00	7/30/2014	-	7/30/2014	Closed Won	-	Closed Won

Notice the color code in the report value. It will turn green when the number or date gets higher or newer respectively, and red for the other way round. For the text field, if the value changes it will turn orange.

Let's perform another use case: the management wants to analyze all open pipelines with the **Stage** value not moving in the last three months. You need to perform the following steps:

1. Create a new report and select opportunities with **Historical Trending** as the report type.

2. Grab all the fields as required and drop them into the **Report Builder** area.

3. Add report filter - Stage not equal to **Closed Won, Closed Lost**.

4. Add another report filter - **Amount** greater than 0.

5. Add **Historical Field Filter**, where **Stage (Historical) 3 Months Ago** equals **Stage**.

6. Select **Historical Date** as **1 Month Ago**, **2 Months Ago**, and **3 Months Ago**.

7. Run the report and see the result.

Filtered By: Edit
 Stage (Historical) 3 Months Ago equals **Stage** Clear
 AND **Stage** not equal to **Closed Won,Closed Lost** Clear
 AND **Amount** greater than 0 Clear

Historical Date: 1 Month Ago, 2 Months Ago, 3 Months Ago

Account Name: Account Name	Opportunity Name ↑	Stage		Stage (Historical)			Amount		Amount (Historical)		
		Today	9/28/2014	10/28/2014	11/28/2014		Today	9/28/2014	10/28/2014	11/28/2014
Ace Iron and Steel Inc.	Ace Iron and Steel Inc.-	Needs Analysis	Needs Analysis	Needs Analysis	Needs Analysis		$48,000.00	$48,000.00	$48,000.00	$48,000.00
Batman 1	Batman-Nickel Soda	Prospecting	Prospecting	Prospecting	Prospecting		$18,000.00	-	-	-
OCBC	Blues Entertainment Corp.-	Prospecting	Prospecting	Prospecting	Prospecting		$13,000.00	$13,000.00	$13,000.00	$13,000.00
Edge Communications 2	Edge Hell	Qualification	Qualification	Qualification	Qualification		$900.00	$900.00	$900.00	$900.00
Emerson Transport	Emerson Transport-Extra SG	Prospecting	Prospecting	Prospecting	Prospecting		$5,000.00	$5,000.00	$5,000.00	$5,000.00
FlowCo Inc	FlowCo Inc-Additional	Prospecting	Prospecting	Prospecting	Prospecting		$5,800.00	$5,800.00	$5,800.00	$5,800.00
FlowCo Inc	Flow NY 200K	Qualification	Qualification	Qualification	Qualification		$10,850.00	$850.00	$850.00	$10,850.00
Haha Man	Haha Man-SF Implementation	Prospecting	Prospecting	Prospecting	Prospecting		$10,000.00	-	-	-
Jackson Controls	Jackson Controls-	Prospecting	Prospecting	Prospecting	Prospecting		$5,000.00	$5,000.00	$5,000.00	$5,000.00
Adil Corp	TEST2	Qualification	Qualification	Qualification	Qualification		$160,000.00	$160,000.00	$160,000.00	$160,000.00
	Test 2A	Needs Analysis	Needs Analysis	Needs Analysis	Needs Analysis		$101,500.00	$101,500.00	$101,500.00	$101,500.00

Objects related to historical trending

When you enable an object for historical trending, just like the case of field history, Salesforce will create a new object to store historical data. For standard objects, it will end with __hd, for example, Opportunity__hd. For custom objects, it will be _hd, for example, Claim__c_hd.

If you want to understand how the historical trending data is stored at the backend, check out the following paragraphs. If not, you can skip to the *Limitations of historical trending* subsection.

For each field track, Salesforce will create two fields to track its value:

- For an existing value, this field will end with __hpr, for example, Amount__hpr

- For a new value, this field will end with __hst, for example, Amount__hst

For a custom field, for example, it will be Margin__c_hpr and Margin__c_hst.

A few other important fields in this object are as follows:

- ParentId: This is the record being tracked

- ValidFromDate: This is the start date for a value

- ValidToDate: This is the end date for a value

If you are familiar with SOQL, you can run this query:

```
SELECT Id, ParentId, ValidFromDate, ValidToDate, Amount__hpr,
Amount__hst, CloseDate__hpr, CloseDate__hst,
ForecastCategoryName__hpr, ForecastCategoryName__hst,
Probability__hpr, Probability__hst, StageName__hpr,
StageName__hst, CreatedById, CreatedDate FROM Opportunity__hd
WHERE ParentId = '0065000000MztiBAAR' ORDER BY CreatedDate
```

The same applies to the field history object; you will not be able to create or update the value in this field manually, and also the permission to delete is not allowed.

Limitations of historical trending

The limitations of historical trending are as follows:

- It is only valid for **Opportunity**, **Case**, and **Forecasting Item** (for collaborative forecast only).

- At most, three objects are allowed for custom objects.

- At most, eight fields are allowed for each object. This count includes the fields always enabled for **Opportunity** and **Forecasting Item**.

- At most, five historical snapshots are allowed for each historical trending report.

- You can only select a maximum of **First Day 3 Months Ago** for the **Historical Date** value.

- There are up to four historical field filters on each historical trend report.

Selecting features

We have seen many features in Salesforce related to accessing historical data, and we also discussed each of them in detail. But how should we select which features that suit our needs?

You may implement more than one feature as a solution. Let's take a few use cases to decide which features to choose.

The first use case will be for showing the history of change of the account owner in the account page layout.

For this use case, we can implement field history tracking on **Account Owner**. Enable tracking account history and select **Account Owner**. Ensure that the list related to **Account History** is added to the account page layout. Once this is enabled, when someone changes **Account Owner**, the old and the new account owners will be seen, including information of when the change happened and the user who made the change.

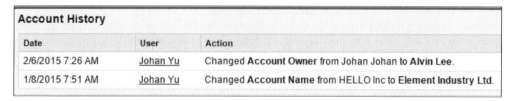

Let's see the second use case. Continuing the first use case, we would like to extend tracking to Chatter feeds.

You can enable feed tracking to track the same fields, but the fields tracked in the Chatter feeds do not relate with the fields tracked in field history tracking.

So, enable feed tracking on **Account** and select the account owner. The same information in **Account History** will be shown in **Account Feed** when you enable field history tracking. Since this is a feed, other users have access to the account, and they are able to comment, like, bookmark, and add topics to the feed.

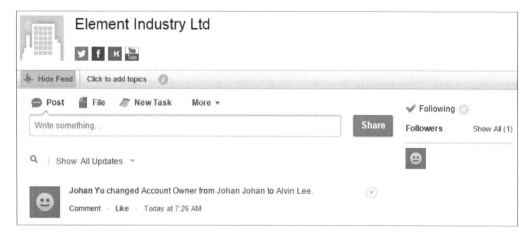

If you are the person who changed the account owner, the feed will show up in your Chatter feed. Users who follow you will see this in their feed on the **Home** page, including e-mail notifications if the user configured to receive e-mails.

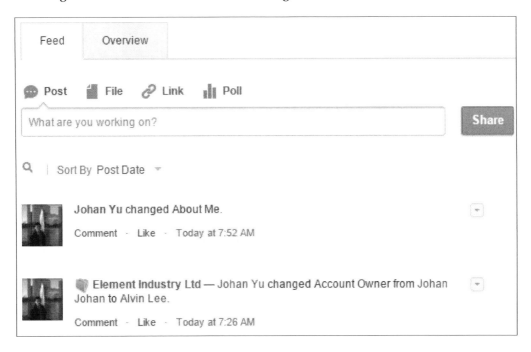

Moving to our third use case: we want to show the total amount of opportunities for each stage and every day in historical data.

We can configure a reporting snapshot to run daily to store the total amount for each stage, but the amount will be recorded only after the reporting snapshot is scheduled. Once it is run for a few days, we can run a report to the target object to see the data.

This is a sample of a report that uses a reporting snapshot, where we can see the total amount of change every day by stage:

Date ↑	Amount
Pipeline Stage: Prospecting (3 records)	
2/1/2015	$415,000.00
2/2/2015	$315,000.00
2/3/2015	$315,000.00
Pipeline Stage: Qualification (3 records)	
2/1/2015	$135,000.00
2/2/2015	$185,000.00
2/3/2015	$185,000.00

Our fourth use case is as follows: the sales manager would like to monitor the entire pipeline of his sales representatives, and show **Stage** and **Amount** changes for the last three months.

Let's use the historical trending report to show each opportunity stage development and changes in the amount for the opportunity over time.

Historical Date: 1 Month Ago, 2 Months Ago, 3 Months Ago								
Opportunity Name ↑	Amount	Amount (Historical)			Stage	Stage (Historical)		
	Today	11/7/2014	12/7/2014	1/7/2015	Today	11/7/2014	12/7/2014	1/7/2015
Flow Co Inc-Additional	$5,800.00	$5,800.00	$5,800.00	$5,800.00	Qualification	Prospecting	Prospecting	Prospecting
Flow NY 200K	$10,850.00	$850.00	$10,850.00	$10,850.00	Qualification	Qualification	Qualification	Qualification
Golden Still Org	$10,000.00	-	$10,000.00	$10,000.00	Qualification	-	Qualification	Qualification

Using the historical trending report, we will see the changes in each record over time. As shown in the preceding screenshot, the current stage for **Flow Co Inc-Additional** is **Qualification**, while for the last month, it is still **Prospecting**. For the **Flow NY 200K** opportunity, the amount has changed from **$850.00** to **$10,850.00** in two months.

Summary

We discussed multiple options used to access historical data without looking at backing up files. However, all options need you to enable and configure before it starts tracking.

Field history tracking will be the most convenient way when you need to audit value changes over time to the fields. Users are not allowed to create or modify the value. Feed tracking has almost similar tracking to field history tracking, feed tracking is more for collaboration with your team, where users following the record will be notified, and they are able to make comments in Chatter feeds.

Scheduling reporting snapshots at a daily or weekly frequency will capture data for that time, so you will be able to analyze the data captured in the custom object later on. Historical trending is the latest technology offered by Salesforce out of the box, where you are able to watch the data change over time. One of the good use cases to use historical trending is that a manager can easily monitor his team's opportunity pipeline progress.

In the next chapter, we will discuss the Salesforce1 mobile app. Users are able to use this out-of-the-box app in smartphones. We will discuss how to use dashboards and reports in the Salesforce1 mobile app.

9

Dashboards and Reports in Salesforce1

This chapter will show you how to access your dashboards and reports from your smart phone using the newest Salesforce mobile app, "Salesforce1". We will not go through the details of Salesforce1 app installation, permissions, configuration, notifications, actions, approvals, events, and navigations. But we will discuss accessing dashboards and reports with Salesforce1 in depth, including access from a mobile web browser.

We will also discuss another app in brief at the end of this chapter—Salesforce Mobile Dashboards. However, this is not the main app for access to your Salesforce data.

The discussion in this chapter is based on Salesforce1 version 7.1, and the following topics will be covered:

- Introduction to the Salesforce1 app
- Working with dashboards in Salesforce1
- Sharing dashboard snapshots with the Chatter feed
- Working with reports in Salesforce1
- Limitations of Salesforce1
- The Salesforce Mobile Dashboards app

Introduction to the Salesforce1 mobile app

Salesforce1 is an enterprise-class, out-of-the-box mobile app built and supported by Salesforce. It is available for all Salesforce users, including Chatter users. This app is available on both the iOS and Android platforms. You can download and install it for free from the App Store for iOS devices, and from Google Play for Android devices.

This app supports both smartphones and tablets. Salesforce1 is also available for users who use supported web browsers from supported devices. It gives the same user experience as installed app. With this, you don't need to install an app on your mobile device.

The app will work for you out of the box and respect your Salesforce configuration and customization implemented, without any efforts to reconfigure it, with exception of packages installed from AppExchange which are not certified for Salesforce1, including Visualforce pages not designed or configured for use in Salesforce1. This app gives you real-time access to the same Salesforce.com information as you access using a web browser.

Prior to the introduction of the Salesforce1 app, Salesforce built different mobile apps such as Salesforce Classic, Salesforce Touch, Logger & Forcepad, and Chatter Mobile. But the Salesforce1 mobile app combined all of these apps into one single platform for a unified mobile experience across iOS and Android smartphones and tablets.

The Salesforce1 mobile app is automatically enabled for all existing and new Salesforce users, unless turned off by your Salesforce administrator. When you log in to Salesforce1, the branding, content, and menu of the app are dependent on your Salesforce configuration and accessibility. The following screenshot shows the interface of this app:

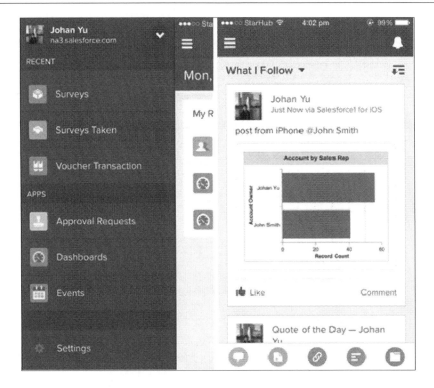

Working with a dashboard in the Salesforce1 app

To access a dashboard in Salesforce1, tap on the navigation menu and scroll down to the **Dashboards** menu under the **APPS** section. You will find the same dashboard as you see on the Salesforce website.

As a minimum, you need the **Run Reports** permission to open a dashboard stored in a dashboard folder. Permission needed to open a dashboard in Salesforce1 is exactly the same with permissions you need to open the dashboard using web browser.

The **Dashboard** menu's visibility in Salesforce1 does not depend on the **Tab Settings** in the user's profile. Once you tap on the **Dashboards** menu, it will open a list of the recent dashboards that you have opened.

To refresh the dashboard from the mobile app, tap on the refresh icon at the bottom of the screen. It will prompt you to confirm the refreshed dashboard.

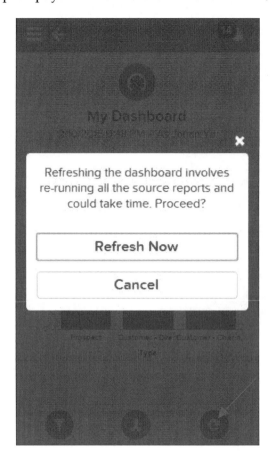

Salesforce1 app version 6.0 and later versions support offline read-only access. You are able to open the most recent dashboards you worked on from the Salesforce1 app. Of course, you cannot refresh it when offline. Offline access to dashboards is not for Salesforce mobile web browser access.

 To enable offline support for the Salesforce1 app, navigate to **Setup | Mobile Administration | Offline** and check **Enable Caching in Salesforce1**. This is only for the Salesforce1 app installed on your devices, not for the Salesforce1 mobile browser app.

Dynamic dashboards

As of the Spring 2015 release, when you open the dynamic dashboard in the Salesforce1 mobile app, and you have permission to run the dashboard as some other user, you will be able to do the same in the mobile app. Tap on the icon to select a user as running user for the dashboard. Note that you need to install the latest Salesforce1 mobile app to support this.

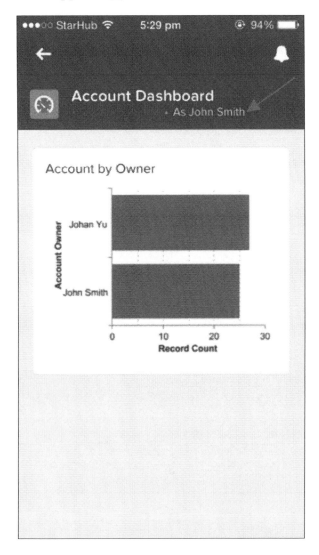

Dashboard filters

The ability to filter dashboards in the Salesforce1 mobile app was introduced in the release of Spring 2015. If your dashboard is configured with filters, you will be able to filter the dashboard in the mobile app. Tap on the filter icon and select the defined filters. Note that you need to install the latest Salesforce1 mobile app to support this as well.

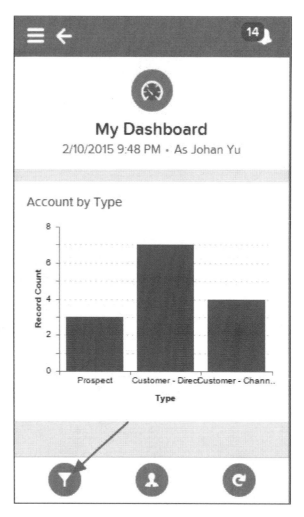

Share a dashboard snapshot with the Chatter feed

If you remember in *Chapter 6*, *Creating Your First Dashboard*, we explained the ability to post dashboard snapshots to the dashboard feed or user/group feed from Salesforce in web browsers. This can be done in the Salesforce1 app as well, by performing these steps:

1. Open the dashboard from the Salesforce1 app.

2. Tap on the dashboard component.

3. Look for the icon in the bottom-right corner of the screen.

4. Tap on the icon and enter text as you need. You can also mention the users with the tap user icon. The users will get an e-mail if Chatter e-mail notification is enabled for **Mentions me in a comment**.

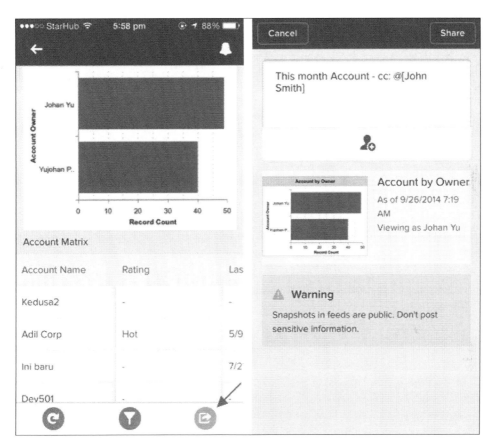

5. When other users see your Chatter page, they will also see the dashboard snapshot in your Chatter feed.

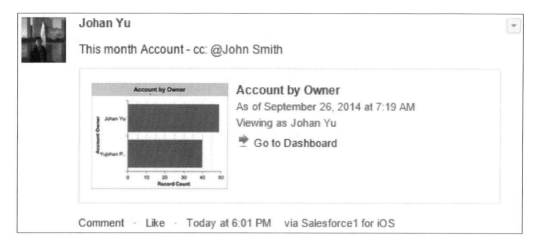

Working with reports in the Salesforce1 app

There are a few options to access reports in the Salesforce1 mobile app. Let's discuss them in detail.

The Reports menu item

Before the spring 2015 release, the **Reports** menu item was not available. If you cannot see the **Reports** menu in the Salesforce 1 app menu, make sure you add the **Reports** menu. Navigate to **Setup | Mobile Administration | Mobile Navigation**, select **Reports**, and add it to the selected items.

When you open a report in the Salesforce1 mobile app, the report format will be ignored. The summary and matrix reports data are presented in columns, with each summary field being in its own column. You can sort the report by tapping on the header of a column. By default, this will sort the report with that column in ascending order, tap the header again to sort in descending order.

Drill down from the dashboard

As you know, a report is one of the options used as a data source for a dashboard. When you tap on the dashboard component in the Salesforce1 mobile app, it will drill down to the report used as the data source. When the report opens, it will show the dashboard component on top of the report, although there is no chart defined in the original report. If the original report has a chart added to it, the original chart will not show in the Salesforce1 mobile app.

You can filter data in this report based on dashboard grouping by tapping on the group in a chart of the report, except for the table and matrix components. When you tap on an item of the chart in the report shown in the following screenshot, it will pop up and show a summary for that group, and the data in the report shown below the summary will be filtered by that grouping. You will notice that the filter icon at the bottom will show **1**. When you tap on that icon, it will show that the report is currently filtered by a value. It will also show a button that can be used to remove all of the filtering.

Chatter feed or group

Just like dashboards, reports can be posted to a Chatter group or your Chatter feed. Users will be able to click on the URL from the Salesforce1 mobile app. The report displayed will be the same as what you see when you open the report from the **Reports** menu.

Limitations of the Salesforce1 app

There are a few limitations when accessing dashboards and reports from the mobile app, but since this app is used for on-the-go access, you need not have all the features of dashboards and reports on a small-screen device.

Here is a summary of some of the limitations:

- Users are not able to create and edit a dashboard or report
- The report format may be ignored, and drill-down may go to tabular, summary, or matrix reports
- The drill-down setting in the dashboard component may not work
- The chart added in the report may not show up
- Chatter feeds are not available in dashboard and report

The Salesforce Mobile Dashboards app

Salesforce Mobile Dashboards is another out-of-the-box app from Salesforce.com. It can be used to access Salesforce dashboards and reports. This is not the same app as Salesforce1; it is older than Salesforce1. There has been no further development or enhancement on this app.

This app is only for iPads and is available in the App Store for free. You need to enable it by navigating to **Setup | Mobile Administration | Mobile Dashboards | Settings** and selecting **Enable the Mobile Dashboards iPad app for all users**.

You will not find a list of reports in this app, but you can access it from the dashboard where the report is used as a data source. Just as in the Salesforce1 app, you will be able to drill down the dashboard components to a report and filter the report by a component group using this app. When you launch the app for the first time, it will ask for login credentials. Then it will show you the recent dashboards you've worked with, you can also search using the dashboard name.

Go through the list of dashboards and tap to open.

Tap on the chart in the dashboard to open a bigger chart. Tapping on the grouping area will show you the value of the group summary. Tapping the area twice will open the chart with the reports used as data sources. Just as in the Salesforce1 app, the reports will be shown in tabular format. The original reports will not show up. You are able to sort the report by tapping on the report header.

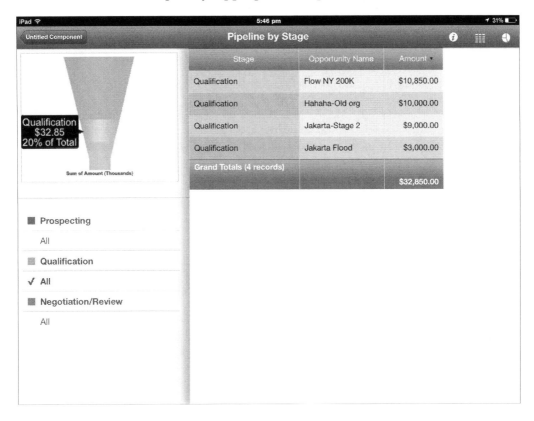

Summary

We started this chapter with an introduction to the Salesforce1 mobile app, continued by working with dashboards, and explained about dynamic dashboards and the dashboard filter using the Salesforce1 mobile app. We also discussed the ability to post dashboard snapshots to our Chatter feed for collaboration.

Next, we discussed the brand new **Report** menu , which introduced by Salesforce in Spring 2015 release. We also discussed an additional filter feature when drilling down reports from dashboard components. Then we summarized the limitations when accessing dashboards and reports from the mobile app. Finally, we discussed another app called Salesforce Mobile Dashboards in brief to end this chapter.

This is the last chapter for this book. Thanks for reading and learning! We hope this will help you in your daily job as a Salesforce.com system administrator or a business user to fully utilize the reporting features of Salesforce.com.

Index

Thank you for buying
Salesforce Reporting and Dashboards

About Packt Publishing

Packt, pronounced 'packed', published its first book, *Mastering phpMyAdmin for Effective MySQL Management*, in April 2004, and subsequently continued to specialize in publishing highly focused books on specific technologies and solutions.

Our books and publications share the experiences of your fellow IT professionals in adapting and customizing today's systems, applications, and frameworks. Our solution-based books give you the knowledge and power to customize the software and technologies you're using to get the job done. Packt books are more specific and less general than the IT books you have seen in the past. Our unique business model allows us to bring you more focused information, giving you more of what you need to know, and less of what you don't.

Packt is a modern yet unique publishing company that focuses on producing quality, cutting-edge books for communities of developers, administrators, and newbies alike. For more information, please visit our website at www.packtpub.com.

About Packt Enterprise

In 2010, Packt launched two new brands, Packt Enterprise and Packt Open Source, in order to continue its focus on specialization. This book is part of the Packt Enterprise brand, home to books published on enterprise software – software created by major vendors, including (but not limited to) IBM, Microsoft, and Oracle, often for use in other corporations. Its titles will offer information relevant to a range of users of this software, including administrators, developers, architects, and end users.

Writing for Packt

We welcome all inquiries from people who are interested in authoring. Book proposals should be sent to author@packtpub.com. If your book idea is still at an early stage and you would like to discuss it first before writing a formal book proposal, then please contact us; one of our commissioning editors will get in touch with you.

We're not just looking for published authors; if you have strong technical skills but no writing experience, our experienced editors can help you develop a writing career, or simply get some additional reward for your expertise.

Salesforce CRM: The Definitive Admin Handbook

Second Edition

ISBN: 978-1-78217-052-5   Paperback: 426 pages

A Comprehensive guide for the setup, configuration, and customization of Salesforce CRM

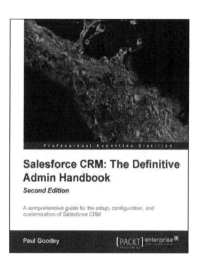

1. Updated for Spring '13, this book covers best practice administration principles, real-world experience, and critical design considerations for setting up and customizing Salesforce CRM.

2. Analyze data within Salesforce by using reports, dashboards, custom reports, and report builder.

3. A step-by-step guide offering clear guidance for the customization and administration of the Salesforce CRM application.

Salesforce CRM Admin Cookbook

ISBN: 978-1-84968-424-8   Paperback: 266 pages

Over 40 recipes to make effective use of Salesforce CRM with the use of hidden features, advanced user interface techniques, and real-world solutions

1. Implement advanced user interface techniques to improve the look and feel of Salesforce CRM.

2. Discover hidden features and hacks that extend standard configuration to provide enhanced functionality and customization.

3. Build real-world process automation, using the detailed recipes to harness the full power of Salesforce CRM.

Please check **www.PacktPub.com** for information on our titles

Developing Applications with Salesforce Chatter

ISBN: 978-1-78217-116-4   Paperback: 130 pages

Leverage the power of Chatter to boost collaboration in your organization

1. Understand Salesforce Chatter and its architecture.

2. Configure and set up Chatter for your organization.

3. Improve Chatter features by utilizing Apex and Visualforce Pages.

4. Discover the new Chatter REST API for developers.

Salesforce.com Customization Handbook

ISBN: 978-1-84968-598-6   Paperback: 454 pages

Customize Salesforce to automate your business requirements

1. Learn the concepts of Salesforce.com to automate business processes.

2. Streamline your sales process and improve collaboration in your organization.

3. A step-by-step approach to online course design to make your business more reliable and productive.

Please check **www.PacktPub.com** for information on our titles

Made in the USA
San Bernardino, CA
26 April 2020